Games Women Play: A Sexual Primer in Female Motives

Raymond Riley

Chapter One

THE PREGNANCY GAME

Every female has a choice of games. A woman plays the game according to age, class, marital status, education, financial condition.

A college coed might find it altogether appropriate to overtly initiate a sexual relationship. An older woman might prefer to encourage the man subtly; and a wealthy woman might take to being seen at the best places and so indicate her availability. But no matter what the ploy, the long and even the shortrange aim is precisely the same: to bed a man. either in or out of marriage.

If the goal is to take a man to bed. then does it matter whether or not a man knows the rules?

It just isn't so that every woman's ultimate goal is marriage. As Janice Glover wrote in Sense and Sensibility for Single Women, 'That old bit about a woman wanting a whole loaf or none when it comes to a man is, in my single judge ment, so much malarkey. The truth is that there are a good many single women who would have a hunk of tasty fruit cake which they must share with other women than a whole spongecake for themselves.1

Although Miss Glover's selection of caketype may have been unfortunate, due to the connotations of 'fruit', what she really means is that not all single women want a guy to say 'I do'. It may be sufficient if he's willing to bed, board, comfort, and caress her.

Most every book ever written about the sex habits of single girls in all walks of life contributes to the games women play. Although men are slowly catching up, there is no doubt that women are the most expert at sexual gamesmanship.

Women's games are played with many props: false eyebrows, false eyelashes, false breasts, false fingernails, and even false bottoms. Most American men expect these artificial accessories.

The oldest game, played by women around the world, can be identified simply by the statement, 'I'm pregnant'

The Pregnancy Game is played by the amateur lover, the professional manseeker, the factory worker, and the college girl, and by the young and the old (well, not too old). The Group for the Advancement of Psychiatry in Sex and the College Student puts it this way, 'A girl is more likely to expose herself to pregnancy if she generally tends to live out unconscious wishes in an impulsive manner.'

A chick who wants to make the scene and catch a guy for good might be willing to make him think she forgot to take her pill. With contraception left more and more to the girl, she finds herself in the position of controlling the rules of The Pregnancy Game.

How would a guy charged with being the errant father know for sure? How can he tell whether or not he is the one really responsible? Can he duck out morally, legally or socially? If he does marry her and she turns out not to be pregnant how deep will he be into this marriage? The choices suggested by The Pregnancy Game have deeper roots than some of the other games where the man's only struggle is to get out. When The Pregnancy Game is successful the girl can always say after the wedding: the doctor made a mistake, she miscalculated or missarried. But he's caught. She can, of course, easily deny she ever told him she was pregnant, to avoid a possible annulment.

A well-heeled knowledgeable fellow can hand the girl some cash and tell her to find a willing doctor. Some others might go on the offensive and play The Counter Pregnancy Game. That's what Ronald K. did. (His name as well as the others referred to in this and other chapters have been changed).

Ronald was appearing in a popular summerstock theatre. It was his first year with the company but he had already built a reputation as a mysterious, enigmatic character. It was rumored that he had a winter home in the south of France. Dark and handsome and in his late twenties, it was also whispered that he was a deposed Egyptian prince, a descendant of a Turkish emperor and/or the son of a mysterious English nobleman. In truth he had been bom of White Russians who had escaped after the revolution.

He had an independent private income and merely enjoyed summer theatre as a diversion.

Ronald's cosmopolitan manner, his continental accent, his good looks and apparent affluence made it easy for him to attract women, and he became a target for the younger girls who made up the company.

One young girl, who told herself that she was going to land Ronald, was spending her first summer with the company, on vacation from college. Lisa, just turned twenty, came from a small southern town outside of Atlanta. She was used to encouraging young men with a swish of her backside or a French kiss. She knew just how far to take a young man before jumping out of the car and rushing into her house. On occasion she allowed herself to spend a night discreetly. She knew how to make a boy feel like a man; she knew where to put her mouth, how to grind her thighs into his groin; hold back so that he would come panting after her. She did these things to satisfy her own ego as well as inflame her recurrent hunger. But what she really wanted was for someone to take her to all the romantic places of the world she had read about. She wanted someone with unlimited wealth. Lisa had fantasised that she would meet a prince some day. When she met Ronald she knew he was the man. The problem was, of course, how to get him.

He expressed no interest in her even when she passed him in the hall, sideways, allowing her fullbreasted figure to brush up against his chest; or when she stumbled against him in a scene they were playing together on the stage.

Bab's plan was to have Ronald want her and get her but not right away, not with the appearance of being an easy mark. She didn't want a casual affair. Lisa was looking for a permanent alliance, not a parttime dalliance.

One Sunday afternoon during the second week in June, with nearly three months of the season left, Lisa decided to act. If she were ever to get her game started it would have to begin at once.

Although she had never had trouble at college, Lisa had difficulty getting started now. At college a pair of tight slacks that barely made it over her round, soft bottom, a blouse twisted and knotted just below her burgeoning breasts, her browngold hair loosely flowing over her slightly madeup eyes, moist lipstick that maintained a petulant look and dabs of perfume anointing the proper parts of her anatomy had always been sufficient weapons. But Ronald seemed immune. She wanted him to want her sexually up to the point where she could turn him off. Then it would be easy to get him to propose. That would be the final entrapment.

As they walked in a small park for the first time together, he took her hand. She thought, this is the beginning. She pulled him closer to her, forcing him to bend his arm under her bosom.

'You have such nice, white skin.' He patted her hand. 'You haven't done a hard day's work m your life.'

She leaned her head on his shoulder. 'I really haven't had to.'

Ronald motioned for them to sit under a tree. their backs leaning against the trunk.

They sat quietly for a moment and then Lisa twisted her body so she was able to lay her head in his lap. She held her fingers over his mouth. 'I don't want you to think of anything.'

'Not even you?' he asked. In a sense he was playing the first part of a game he easily recognised. Ronald had nothing to lose. He encouraged her to go on.

She pulled his head down to hers, so that his lips touched hers. tickled the inside of his mouth with her tongue. She knew that prince or fraud, son of an emperor or son of a carpenter ~ he was a man and he would have to respond.

Ronald caressed her breasts, bare under the knotted blouse, allowing his hands to reach down and round her back, cup ping the cool buttocks. At that moment Lisa shattered his mood, pulled herself away and got up.

'Must you go?' he asked almost indifferently.

Playing scene two of the game, she said, 'I have a part to rehearse.' Then she ran off.

Ronald called after her, loud enough for Lisa to hear, 'Bitch.' Lisa heard and laughed because now she felt he would pursue her. She didn't have long to wait.

That night, after the evening performance, Ronald directed her to his room. There were no preliminaries. Although she would have preferred to have him tell her he loved her. that wasn't a necessary part of the game. In allowing Ronald to win the first encounter she would she figured win the final battle.

In bed Ronald was everything she had hoped. He treated her gently, caressing her softly, stroking her into expectation, then backing away as she murmured to have him come to her quickly. He wouldn't and the murmur changed to a cry.

Then he answered her cry. She had never felt the surge of womanhood as she did that night.

The next day she avoided Ronald. This was the accessary and difficult next stage. Finally she told him, 'Ronald. I never should have. It was all my fault. I never should have allowed it to happen.'

She didn't tell him that this was the first time, not expecting him to believe that.

It was important for him to think that her personal shame was an excuse to stay away. It was difficult for her. He found other women as weeks went on. Lisa ached to have him be with her. But she waited until the second week in August for the next stage.

She picked an evening when they could be alone together. He invited her to his room. Ronald sat on the edge of the bed waiting for her to join him. Instead she stood and nervously began, 'Ever since that night, that wonderful night, there's been no one else. I've thought only of you.'

Ronald didn't say anything, just patted the bed. Lisa went on, affecting her best sweet Southern accent, 'I've wondered what you must think of me. But I have to tell you this now because,' she lowered her eyes, 'I'm pregnant.'

Lisa waited, expecting him to profess great care or at least concern. His attitude and expression remained unconcerned. Then he asked simply, 'Are you sure?'

'Oh, yes,' she ran up to him, got on her knees and buried her face in his lap. 'I got the test report from the doctor today. It has to be you. There has been no one else all summer. I, I guess the pill just didn't work.'

Ronald, hardly pushing her away, got up. She almost fell as he walked past her to the bureau. He took a piece of folded paper out of the top drawer and waved it, 'You know what this is?'

'No, I don't,' she said in a littlegirl voice.

Speaking slowly and deliberately, affecting the accent of a European boardingschool student, he told her. This is a medical certificate stating that because of a case of mumps contracted three years ago, I am sterile. That means, young lady, you are either a liar or a fool. In any event I cannot possibly be the father of the little bastard you may or may not be carrying.'

'Oh Ronald,' Lisa started to cry, mostly because The Pregnancy Game was taking an unexpected twist. 'It's not true, I was making it up. I just wanted you to marry me.'

'But,' Ronald waved the paper as she crawled over to him, 'I was not making it up. Now, get out.'

Lisa got up slowly and walked out of the room, not looking back. After she had gone Ronald put his laundry list back in the drawer.

In The Pregnancy Game the man can never really be sure of the truth. It is a chance rule of thumb that if the girl has been bedding with more than one man she's trying them all on for marriageable size. This is not a game to be played by the weak.hearted woman. When the male goes on the offen sive, as Ronald did, all can be too easily lost. Lisa had spent the summer planning while Ronald had spent it playing.

One must not confuse the girl who deliberately feigns pregnancy with the ones such as Don Juan's conquests who felt pregnant when he walked into the room.

Since the United States (unlike France) doesn't permit a girl to marry a dead man, a girl here must go after a very. muchalive father. Under De Gaulle it is possible for a woman to be married to a dead man. In fact, in 1961 a pregnant woman was allowed to be married to her deceased lover.

The aim of The Pregnancy Game is usually marriage.

However, it may have as its goal a lifetime of support. As Dr J. B. Rice wrote in Esquire ' ... her sex by nature inclined to be deceitful, underhanded and tricky.'

For the woman over thirty who has only an evenmoney chance at marriage, the chances of her playing The Preg nancy Game are fewer but, nevertheless, it may often be the last gamble.

Frieda F. was thirtyone, and had never married. She had a fine figure, a betterthanaverage face and features. She tried hard, oh how she tried. She was going with Sam J. a man in his early forties who thought his delightful mghts with Frieda would never be complicated by marriage. She wasn't much good at learning new techniques for the bed but she made a willing student. Sam was successful in business, and he wasn't going to have Frieda his first failure, no matter how long it might take.

Frieda, on the other hand, knew that time was running out on her. In another two or three years she would have great difficulty keeping up a sagging chin, hiding the lines under her eyes, firming the breasts, keeping her figure. She knew Sam was much too shrewd to be taken in by a lie. Even so. she hadn't wanted to deliberately deceive him. Instead she allowed herself to become pregnant. Sam calmly handed her a shaft of bills and told her to find a competent abortionist.

Frieda cried, told Sam she wanted the baby, that it was his child. He told her that that was nonsense.

'You're a beast,' she screamed.

'Beast or not,' he answered, 'I can't let you have the child*

And I can't marry you. I'm already married.'

'I never knew. You never told me,' she sobbed.

'You never asked. You never wanted to know. Why did you have to go and louse up a perfectly good arrangement?'

Sam's matteroffact reply was too much for her. She took the money. Frieda found out that when a woman plays The Pregnancy Game she must know the character of the man with whom she's dealing.

Rowena L., on the other hand, was a pretty young thing, with a welldefined body and a very sharp mind. She knew exactly what to do with both. By the age of twenty she had figured there was more to life than living in Deposit, New York, as the daughter of a dairy farmer. There was also a lot more to life than spending time in the hay, literally, with " the local boys. She read the bigcity papers, knew exactly how to take care of herself. Pregnancy was the last thing she was worried about. It was also to be her first line of attack.

That became apparent to her when she met Skip, the twentythreeyearold son of one of her father's most important customers. Skip was as innocent as any young man could be who allowed himself to be called Skippy. At first Rowena made fun of him. criticised the wideeyed innocent way he looked at her when she sat crosslegged on the floor, her miniskirt climbing to meet her thigh and his eye at the same time. She embarrassed him by brushing against him so that the firm tips of her bosom creased his chest. He came up to the farm with his father at least once a week. Rowena looked forward to seeing him, not because she was aware of his good looks, and that his father was wealthy, but because she could make fun of him.

The idea of seducing him was a natural followthrough to the verbal sport. But with all the fun she had. Skip never became offended. Rowena thought he was not too bright when in fact. he was just uncommonly shy and would never have said anything to her that would sound the remotest bit insulting.

Skip's father encouraged his son to let Rowena show him around the farm and look at the latest electrical milking equipment. He thought it would be important to know that phase of the business.

'Let me show you,' Rowena told him happily, took his reluctant hand and led him away.

He asked her questions about the operations of the farm.

'Do you really care?' she asked.

'Of course; he said, 'it's important that I know everything there is to know.'

'What do you know about girls?' Rowena asked, dancing away. then flopping on to the straw floor, her bare legs kick ing up at him.

He tried not to look at her, and evade her question.

Rowena persisted and taunted him, 'Have you ever taken a girl out?'

'Of course,' he asserted.

I mean really,' she went on, 'I know you live in New York City. Everyone knows your father is loaded. You must be quite a catch for some scheming girl.'

He blushed. 'I go out,' was all he said.

Rowena let it pass. She showed him around, adding, 'You know there wouldn't be any calves if it weren't for the bulls.'

With each succeeding visit Rowena became more personal in her comments. What had started as an innocent flirtation now became almost an obsession for her. Skip represented escape from Deposit, and independent income.

By the sixth visit, the young man was searching for a way to make love. Rowena recognised the symptoms, the perspiring forehead, the tentative attempts to hold her hand, the awkwardness with which he pretended to be reaching for something so he could put an arm around her. Then it happened.

They were alone at a far end of the barn. It was dusk. Rowena recognised the instant as a must. It might pass and she wouldn't have another opportunity. She drew Skip down on to the straw beside her, said nothing but flung herself upon him, reached for his body under his shirt, let him find her legs, her white cool thighs, kept him from talking with her lips and her tongue. He whimpered and almost cried as she released him from the awkwardness of his position, let his body find hers, let his strength ebb into hers, let him reach for her breasts with his mouth, hold them. slobber, slide up and down on her body, almost depart her, she never quite letting him. He throbbed and she expanded his passion until he was overwhelming her and she forgot that she was taking his innocence away.

When they were through he wanted to cry. He apologised for what he had done. This time she didn't answer him with a wise remark but comforted and patted him. So much so, that he was ready again and they lay together.

"You are a man,' was all she could utter.

For weeks Skip tried to avoid her. It was almost two months before Rowena took him aside. What she had to say was simple, direct and to the point. It was also a lie, Tm pregnant'

He responded as she knew he would. I'll marry you.

He didn't know about abortions or trickery. His honor demanded that he marry her. He liked her, maybe loved her. By this time she had developed a fondness for him. It wasn't too difficult for her to play The Pregnancy Game.

The marriage was planned almost immediately. Bom parents willingly agreed and thought it was a fine idea, although Skip's father wondered how his son had ever worked up the nerve to propose.

That evening Rowena and Skip were alone. They were m the barn.

'This is where it began.' she told him, drawing him to the ground.

This time he hesitated less, although he made a short remark that perhaps they should wait until they were married.

'I feel as though we already are.' She opened herself to bun.

This time she had taken no pill, done nothing that would prevent conception, knowing too that even a sixweek delay in the birth of their child would be accepted by the young man who would soon be her husband. Other games are played with more deviousness than by Rowena. with more finesse than by Frieda but that's the next chapter on The Intrigue Game.

Chapter Two

THE INTRIGUE GAME

O f all the games women play, none is more exciting, more stimulating both emotionally and mentally to the participants than The Intrigue Game. Like some masterful chess game each player makes his or her move, calculated to evoke a predicated response in the other. And, of all the women who play The Intrigue Game, none is more adept at it than the divorcee. If she's been married and divorced more than once, so much the better. If her past husbands have been well-known personalities in the theatre, arts, politics or business, better still. If they have been much older men, the aura of intrigue has its most fascinating appeal. And if she is from some obscure European country and speaks with a delightful accent, she is even more effective, Interestingly enough, knowing all the facts, men still allow themselves to be collected by such a woman, adding to her largesse with cash settlement. Alimony has limited use, because it is cut off with the next marriage. Negotiable bonds and diamonds are the type of reward she can show as symbols of her victory in The Intrigue Game.

One would suppose that a successful businessman, used to manipulating milliondollar deals and able to counter the moves of his financial opponents, should be able to handle himself and cut through the veil of intrigue generated by one female, no matter how alluring she may be. The danger, at least for the man in The Intrigue Game, is that he usually succumbs knowing full well what is happening.

The Intrigue Game gets this greatest notoriety when played by star personalities. However, any woman can play it. Most do at one time or another in their lives. It isn't necessary for a woman to have a string of divorces behind her. One will often do very nicely. The most important attitude she must have is to wear her divorce openly, not garishly, but just to prove she's been around; however, the broken marriage was really not her fault. It is constantly implied that the right man can satisfy her and some day she will find him. She creates an aura of unattainability while suggesting that she is the universal courtesan.

The fact that she had been married states absolutely that she is no simple-minded virgin unwilling to be plucked. She wants something in return for her favors, however. That something is usually money.

Although she hints that her divorce settlement was large enough to make her independent there is no doubt, on the other hand, how much she likes a wealthy man.

This game, as with all those that are played, can only succeed with the correct target. There is no point in chasing after an excited but frightened male. A man doesn't instinc tively want to settle down. If scared by the grandeur of a woman's position and wordliness, intrigue will only make him an unresponsive target. No, the woman playing The Intrigue Games picks her prey in the same manner as does a con man who knows you can't cheat an honest man. She goes after the man who thinks he's going to beat her at her own game. As La Rochefoucauld said, 'Flirtation is at the bottom of women's nature, although all do not practice it, some being restrained by fear, others by sense.'

While it is difficult to argue with the French on matters of sex, flirtation is the nearly universal preliminary that sets in motion The Intrigue Game. It can now be played by the secretary as well as the society play girl. Thanks to television the grande dames have exposed their techniques for all who care to copy them. They suggest that if they made it, why can't the girl from a small town in Nebraska? Take the case of Sharon R. This attractive young thing married just after her seventeenth birthday: She had never slept with a man let alone lived with one, before her marriage to a boy a couple of years older. They had a downtown Manhattan apartment

Each continued to work. She was a secretary in an advertis' ing agency. She was used to the men ogling her figure, and innocently able to ward off their suggestions for an after. hours drink. Even though her marriage had difficulty in getting started, she remained faithful, if unfulfilled.

But as time went on her marriage became stifling. She didn't want to be a cleaning housewife on weekends She found they were too broke to go out much. Added to that her young husband was incapable of pleasing her in bed. After a year she got an out-of-state divorce. So at not quite nineteen she was a divorcee. She moved into her own apartment. For a few weeks she didn't date. She wasn't anxious to get involved in another state of insecurity. If anything she was going to find a man with enough to give her what she wanted in the way of the better things of life. Still, the limited pleasure her husband had offered her was missing. Her body ached. She didn't want to sleep with just any man. But she gradually began to pay more attention to the length of her skirt, the perfume she wore, and the cut of her blouse.

Sharon made up her mind she wanted an older man She was not going to be trapped by a married man or another kid. She made sure she was seen sitting in the lobby of the best hotels, accepted dates for premieres at the theatre, was discreet and careful not to get involved. She knew enough to natter an older man, and never, never made fun of anything he did.

A chance conversation with a stranger in a posh bar was not a pickup, it was a meeting. She kept them all out of her apartment, eliminating the married, the joychasers and the underfinanced. Gradually Sharon affected a slight, unidentifiable accent. She never revealed where she worked or, in fact, that she did work. She never discussed her past or her family. In a sense she became an enigma who flattered an older man by going out with him, chastened him by refusing to go to his place or inviting him to hers.

She hinted at a great tragedy in her life. After six months

she found Alex. He was in his late thirties, younger than most of the men she had recently met but oncedivorced, heir to a large estate, classically goodlooking, polite and available.

The Intrigue Game was put into high gear.

Sharon had developed an inner sense of what would make a man respond. She had, in the preceding months, occasionally invited a man into her apartment, but always someone whom she would not see again. He was only there to satisfy her sex needs, fuel her for the game she was playing.

Alex, however, was the man she wanted for keeps. She had mostly to rely on cunning, the basic ingredient in The Intrigue Game.

After four dates with Alex she allowed him to come into her apartment. She poured him an extra-dry martini, served herself a sweet vermouth on the rocks.

'We've had fun together, Sharon.'

She murmured agreement. He edged closer to her on the couch, reaching back to turn out the lights. Sharon allowed him to put his arm around her, to cup the edge of her breasts.

'Finish your drink,' she told him gently, pulling away.

Alex finished his drink, took her glass out of her hand, began to kiss her around the edge of her mouth, on the side of her neck, inside her ear. She pulled up her legs as his hands found her thighs, the white flesh. For almost a moment she forgot the game.

She stopped him. 'I just can't, Alex. It's still too soon.' She /lowered her voice. 'I have so much to forget, darling.' She closed her eyes. She wanted Alex to imagine an awesome past but not to understand, to know that intrigue directed her.

Alex attempted to comfort her. Sharon had demonstrated that she could be affectionate, that she had been about to give herself to him when a horrible memory had come be tween them. No matter how much Alex pleaded she wouldn't tell him what had happened, begged him to leave. But her tone said that she loved him and he should call back the next day.

When he did call she put him off a few days. Then they had dinner and went to his apartment. There was little to say. She permitted him to undress her slowly, carefully. She held on to him, weak and clinging. As he kissed her warm body, burying his head in her lap, she moaned, 'Oh no, Alex, I can't make this mistake again. I can't go through the torment. I'll be no good for you.'

'You will, you will.' He held her from pulling away. He promised her a fulfillment she had never experienced, he promised her marriage. She ran to the corner of the room. He came over and caressed her.

'Not tonight, Alex, tomorrow when I'm calm.' As much as he begged she was firm. Reluctantly he watched her dress and took her home.

The next day everything went quite smoothly. They drove to a neighboring state where a friend of Alex's got him a waiver on a marriage license and they became husband and wife.

Sharon realised that Alex had married her though he had never thought of permanence with any woman because she had won at the game. Although she could tell him she was really in love, what she really loved was the idea of winning.

It didn't matter now whether her marriage to Alex worked or not, she had proved her superiority, A second divorce might in fact make her all the more attractive.

The Intrigue Game, you see, doesn't have to be played by the notorious. It's a game for even the simplest-minded girl.

She can play it single or married. It doesn't always demand marriage as the goal.

Wendy L. lived outside of Philadelphia. She had married a salesman when she was nineteen and now, five years later, was still looking for sexual gratification.

She knew Carl was playing around on his long trips away. But that didn't matter.

She took to entertaining the local delivery boysand once detained the mailman for an extra hour. She offered them more than they expected. She could use her hands and her mouth with more skill than the usual run of girls they'd come into contact with. It got so the house became a marked place. But still these intermittent affairs offered her no sense of total satisfaction.

Wendy was attractively designed with jetblack hair, a slim figure with an unusually full bosom and wide hips, clear white skin.

She persuaded her husband to move to another neighborhood where she was not known. Now she tried a new tact.

She answered the door to a delivery boy wearing a transparent negligee, allowed him a peek, then slammed the door.

She invited vacuum cleaner salesmen in, sat crosslegged,

allowed them a look then told them she wasn't buying. The flow of salesmen became greater and greater but she held herself back, promising much but delivering nothing.

The class of salesmen improved. She began to receive product samples. She encouraged those with gifts to return. And they did. In her basic simplistic fashion Wendy was doing what Sharon had done, what the most famous courtesans of the world have done and are doing right now. It was just that Wendy's goals were more primitive, her desires less complicated, her wants more easily assuaged. She took pleasure in teasing a messenger, hi making an encyclopedia salesman come back again and again, making him spread his

books on the floor, lying down beside him, turning the pages, rolling over so he could see the fullness of her body, then jumping up to say, 'I've got to get supper ready, my husband will be home soon.' She laughed when he hurriedly packed. But she poked her head out of the door and told him to come back the next day, late in the afternoon. She would see her husband off earlier at the airport.

As Mark Caine wrote in The S Man: 'The successful man will go with the girl of his own class and locality.' By the same token the successful woman in The Intrigue Game will play the social counterpart of the man she's after. Wendy got her book salesman while Sharon got her wealthy executive.

To the casual observer it might seem that Wendy was merely echoing her husband's errant habits, but she would have behaved the same if he had never strayed on his business trips. She just had to prove that she could win and continue winning.

Another facet of The Intrigue Game involves the best friend's husband as the choice target for the designing woman. She can be single, married, or many times married. The important thing is that she must conquer. She just has to prove that she is a better woman than the man's present wife.

Take the case of Esther H., a wellknown actress, often mentioned in the papers and gossip columns. She enjoyed a wonderful professional reputation. She had run through five husbands and was currently married. Nevertheless she had her eye on the husband of a onetime good friend, a director she particularly loathed.

He had directed her in one film and made uncomplimentary remarks about her acting. Worse than that his wife had echoed the same sentiments and made sure her comments reached the press.

From that moment on Esther left nothing to chance. She reversed her attitude toward the director, complimented him at every turn, insisted she wanted him to be her director on her next film, told him how much she had learned and that she was a better actress because of him.

Lloyd had been around a long time. He had directed films long before Esther had ever thought of the movies. He had seen literally hundreds of Esthers, listened to the pleas of many, had bedded a number of them. But these affairs were whimsical, an attitude of his trade, a concomitant of the business. Esther, on the other hand, was out to get the husband of a woman whom she publicly called her best friend and mentor.

Esther planned intrigue with the skill of a super spy. She made sure she attended the same parties, gave out the most complimentary comments about Lloyd and his wife to the press so that earlier public images were reversed. When everyone considered Esther and her husband and Lloyd and his wife as the greatest of friends, she struck. It was no trick at all to get Lloyd to spend time coaching her dramatically. What is more, Lloyd's wife was completely devoid of suspicion. The situation was ideal.

However, Esther wanted more than just a onetime affair, she wanted to hook Lloyd completely. She found from a willing gossip that his wife was averse to being anything more than formal in her bed manners. Lloyd with a few drinks and encouragement from his 'best' friend Esther was more than willing to discuss his wife's sexual inadequacies, 'But I only tell you this because you're a dear friend,' he said between drinks.

They were alone in the library of Esther's Bel Air home after a party which most of the guests had departed. Esther's husband had taken Lloyd's wife home. She had become sick after taking some extra strong drinks that Esther had con- veniently prepared.

Lloyd was ripe for solace and for learning. And Esther was ready to teach the older man.

'Does she do this?' Esther asked, as she rubbed her hand down and up Lloyd's leg, stopping only long enough to make his masculinity assert itself.

'No,' he slurred, 'after aU these years it's always up to me.'

'And this?' Esther continued, as she bit him on the ear,

then reached her hand under his shirt, slowly massaging his chest.

'No,' this time it came out a sigh.

Esther had made him ready. She kissed his readiness, held him in her hand. let her tongue flow over his body as she undressed him, caressing each part of his bared skin and body with her tongue, holding him back so that he would reach for her.

She allowed him to undress her, first her dress, then her bra and panties.

'Does she let you do this?'

This time he didn't answer, rather pushed his body close to her. She played with him, let him try to find her and miss. She turned her back to him and he had a devil of a time reaching around and under, finding where he should go, then taking the right road.

'Does she make it so easy for you?' Esther asked.

'Oh no, no,' he blurted.

Moments, many moments later, after the most exhilarating time he had ever spent, he told her, 'You're wonderful.'

He asked to meet her the next day.

'Why wonderful,' she said, 'we'll have lunch and be sure to bring your wife.'

As the weeks went on Esther was all sweetness and light toward Lloyd's wife. Yet the other woman knew, or at least suspected what was going on. She tried to complain, hint to the press, but no one really believed her. No one could under stand that sweet, changed, happily married Esther had so bound up Lloyd that he couldn't stay away.

There would be only one chance for Lloyd's wife to unhook her husband. That would be to find Esther another man, one who represented a challenge. But what the woman didn't realise was that she, not Lloyd, was the challenge.

Esther was a master of intrigue, of setting up a situation that enabled her to get away with seduction, to make the plot irresistible and the solution complicated.

Maybe Esther enjoyed the sheer satisfaction of sex. Certainly that. but more. She enjoyed winning where she thought others would think she would have no chance. That's what made her dangerous and interesting too.

The Intrigue Game can be played with scents and lotions, with incense and dim lights. Burning candles and soft music can create and preserve an enchanting glow. It is no acci dent that sexual activity can be more easHy induced after a perfect meal in such surroundings.

The girl who invites a man to her apartment and creates the proper setting may be innocently participating in The Intrigue Game. But innocence is shortlived. She is as guilty as the woman who plans a concerted campaign. The ultimate goal is entrapment.

It may be that the quarry secretly wants to be caught Knowing all the facts he can determine whether or not the price is too high, if it isn't too late for him to stop.

If intrigue disturbs him, makes him cautious, he may be less prepared for The Innocence Game.

Chapter Three

THE INNOCENCE GAME

Preoccupation with chastity is certainly not unique to Western peoples. There has hardly been a time or place in recorded history when a woman's virginity (or lack of it) has not been a subject for serious discussion. It should be immediately noted that young girls and older women have gone to great pains to maintain the illusion of chastity. A rather common practice in France and Italy was for the in discreet bride to insert a membrane of animal blood inside her vagina on the wedding night. The unsuspecting groom was therefore able to satisfy himself that he was the first to penetrate his bride. One practice was to display a stained sheet before the townspeople as proof positive of his bride's purity.

Throughout history men have been preoccupied with giving tests of the most bizarre nature to determine a woman's chasteness. Philippe of Navarre in the thirteenth century maintained that the only quality necessary in women was a state of chastity,

The young American girl has learned to act surprised by a pass, feign anger at a kiss and generally attempt to make a man's approach just the slightest bit difficult. The man who believes his girl has never been had by any other man either wants to believe it or he has so much conceit that he thinks he's the only one capable of seducing her. No matter what the reason, he is playing right into her hands.

Entrapment, alone, is not necessarily the only result of the successfully played Innocence Game. Chances are the man will end up with a completely different package from what he expected. By then it will probably be too late to get off scotfree.

Don't think that The Innocence Game is something that an older girl or woman turns to as a last resort. It's something that girls are encouraged to play from the very first date. In a book generally directed at high.schoolage youngsters Judith Unger Scott gives this advice to girls in The Book of Dating: 'When such a boy wants to take you home, the answer should be an unequivocal negative but it need not be put harshly. You can let him know you'd like to see more of him and still convey that you are particular about the company you keep ...' and she goes on to advise to let him know 'You're no easy pickup... but you also would like to know him better ...' For goodness' sake, what it seems the author is really advising, is how to start life with men by playing The Innocence Game. Appear wide-eyed and aghast when any hand attempts to touch your breasts and while you look as if you're going to slam the door in his face, tell him where the key is.

The Innocence Game may be the most deadly of all.

It's one thing for a homely girl to play The Innocence Game. With her it may merely be the rationale for not get ting invited out. But when a good-looking girl with a rounded figure, wiggle-my-way-bottom, and trim legs who has taken to wearing a peek-a-boo micro-miniskirt plays it, watch out!

At 21, Ellen Jane B. was all that, plus a Sassoon haircut that bisected a small oval face. Twiggy eyes and a burlesque measurement bosom. There was nothing innocentlooking about her. Nor was there anything remotely innocent in her social habits. She literally devoured every aspect of life.

Ellen Jane had left home in the Western part of Massachusetts to come to Boston to study to be a secretary. She became a good one, too, in a downtown advertising agency.

She had her own apartment in one of Beacon Street's old brownstones. If she were less than intelligent she might never have questioned the direction her life was taking; she would just have thoroughly enjoyed the dates and the exuberance with which she gave herself to any man who had enough money for dinner and bathed himself regularly. She suspected she was a nymphomaniac but rightly dismissed that notion in favor of one that suggested she was just looking for answers. And her search caused her to experiment.

With Charles: 'Let me kiss you here. Now stay quiet* And she got on her knees before him, allowing the young man to cup her bosom, while she performed fellatio. And when she was through she sent him home. She never saw him again.

With Tony: 'Oh, oh, harder, harder. No, don't stop, don't. It doesn't hurt.' She clenched her teeth and then, rather than scream, bit him on the shoulder. She never saw him again, either.

After driving dozens of men out of her life, Ellen Jane decided to change her style. She dropped her skirt length, wore more conventional hose, permitted herself discreet makeup without exaggerated eyes, let her hah: grow longer and softly waved. She didn't hesitate to wear eyeglasses when working. She passed Tony on the street in her new garb. He looked straight at her and gave no sign of recognition.

Although her body ached for a man and her ego demanded attention, the greater drive to play The Innocence Game to successful completion dominated her moves. The men in the office stopped casting hints as to her availability. She had never had any strong relationships with other girls but now she found it less difficult to be called upon to be the 'other girl' on a blind date. She rightly suspected that a lack of noticeable charm made other girls consider her no competition. The fellows she met were, by her standards, dull and uninteresting. That didn't prevent them from starting a goodnight pass or not too subtly suggesting they'd like to come into her apartment for night maneuver. Ellen Jane

countered a groping hand with a handshake; a proposition r with a totally evasive answer. In a matter of weeks after she started playing The Innocence Game her reputation was as spotless as the swans that swarm in the Boston Public

Gardens pool.

One calm, quiet Sunday morning, while walking down Tremont Street, across from Boston Common, Ellen Jane wondered to herself whether this new pose would ever be profitable. There were few other strollers.

Some sailors on leave from the Navy Yard hardly gave her a glance. Ellen Jane turned to look back at the sailors. Am I that unappealing she wondered? As she turned, the heel of her shoe caught in a crack in the sidewalk. She let out a yelp, loud enough for one of the sailors to turn and run back, catching her before she hit the cement pavement.

Once he had determined that she was okay he told his buddies to go on.

He introduced himself. Roger R. from Peoria, Illinois,

Ellen Jane's first inclination was to brush him off. She saw his peachfuzz beard, and although he was tall and delicately handsome, she didn't figure him to be more than twenty.

Thus hardly marriageable.

'I'm here on leave. I didn't know anyone in Boston.'

His line was so innocent she believed him.

'I was just on my way back from church,' she lied.

He asked and she agreed that he could walk with her. He talked about his home, the small brewery his father owned, the cars he drove, the prep school he had attended. The more he talked the more she was grateful that she hadn't obeyed 'her initial impulse to seduce him. Or all of the sailors. She let him walk her home, blushingly gave him her phone'number. He said his ship was in for repairs and he would be around for a few weeks.

The following weekend he called and they went rollerskating. He held her hand and kissed her on the cheek. The next morning, Sunday, he surprised her and suggested they spend the day together. Ellen Jane agreed.

Sitting on the Common, Roger told her, 'I've never met a girl as sweet as you.'

Ellen Jane smiled. To herself she thought, he's calling me a virgin. For the first time in weeks she felt The Innocence Game was going to pay off. Roger held her hand in his lap. She felt his manhood express itself, stood up hastily and suggested that he see her the following week. The following Saturday he called, said he was tired, could they stay in? Coming from anyone else Ellen Jane would have suspected a ploy. When Roger asked it sounded harmless.

She served him a light wine. He told her he knew she didn't drink.

He talked about marriage to a sweet girl, someone he would be proud to take home, someone who would be able to appreciate everything he and his family had to offer. There was only one drawback.

Roger put his arm around her, reluctantly took it away. 'I'm almost twentyone,' he whispered, 'and I don't know what it is to be a man. I don't know whether I could be a good husband. I don't know.'

Ellen Jane thought she heard a sob in his voice. She suddenly felt sorry for him, not patronisingly, but kindly. She snuggled close so that his limp hand fell cupping her breast She held her breath, then felt his fingers gently close around her. She turned and pulled his face to her, opened her moist mouth, encouraged his tongue to caress its inside.

'Oh, darling; she told him,I'll help you.'

Roger pushed her gently back. She helped him undress her, then she turned her head as he got out of his clothes.

He had turned off the light. The night moon reflected the anxiety on his young, perspiring face. Ellen Jane guided him to her, helping him become a part of her, holding him back. then bringing him closer. Roger grabbed her shoulders and fitfully hung on as his body jerked in paroxysms of expectation. Exhausted he fell across her. Ellen Jane patted his moist hair, gently rolled him off. In a moment she was asleep, dreaming of Peoria, the prize of The Innocence Game.

When she awakened, it was the early part of the morning. Roger was gone. She found an unsigned note pinned tothe pillow. It told her simply that he had to sail that day. That was all.

Ellen Jane beat the pillow with her fist. She started to cry in anger. She had been had and knew it. When a girl plays The Innocence Game, she should know you can't cheat an honest man.

There is, of course. The Innocence Game played by the chaste, the pure and, often the frightened, frustrated and forgiving. Most every advertisement for cosmetics and lotions, toothpastes and underarm deodorants promises to give a girl something she has never had, a sexual orgasm. The countless books on how to get a man, what to wear, how to act, drive relentlessly toward the same goal.

Of course neither the advertisements nor the books come right out and say what the ultimate result will be. But ihe giris know. They can be titillated through reading by

promises of heretofore unknown pleasures without com
promising their virtue.

Arlene Dahl in her book Always Ask a Man has a chapter
on 'Instant Sex.' In it she says, among other interest ing
jewels, that just because he spends money, don t think a girl
has to 'pay back by inviting him in for a nightcap . . . He'll
appreciate you more if you put a high value on your. self,
on your integrity . . . Replace instant sex with instant allure
and its romantic promise....'

Promise of what? That's what twenty eight year old
Francie L. had to find out. By any standards Francie was
plainlooking. She had a rugged, square face that went with
the northern Mhinesota country people. She wore severely
cut clothes and took care of her farmer father.

But this day she was in Minneapolis on a shopping trip.
It was the time of the annual Aquatennial. There was so
much life and carryingon that she felt part of some large,
public picnic. She had placed the order for equipment her
father desired and now wanted to do something for herself.

She went into one of the largest department stores to the
Young Miss department. She fingered the dresses, admired
the scanty skirts, brief bathing suits and grinned sheepishly
at the transparent bras and lacetrimmed panties. She could
afford to wear a lacetrimmed bra with a bow in the center
even if she couldn't parade around in a miniskirt, because
of toopowerful legs. She stood at the counter, staring at the
display, unaware that a salesman for a brassiere manufacturer
was watching her. He had come out of the office and noticed
Francie, because she was eyeing a garment his company
made.

'That's a good bra,' he said matter of factly.

Francie heard the man's voice, turned and blushed. She was definitely unused to buying bras in front of men. She saw a tall man. His voice was pleasant and his looks not at all unkind.

He laughed, 'I've never seen a girl blush so much. You know,' he spoke unemotionally as if he needed to calm her down. 'I sell that brand. Most of the salesmen are men. I mean the store buyers are usually women but the companies send men out on the road to sell them. I wonder why?'

'Maybe they're better salesman,' she offered.

He introduced himself: George W. from Chicago, single and on the road for two weeks and tired, so 'How about a cup of coffee?'

She said. yes and they went into a nearby cafeteria.

George told her, 'I've never seen a girl with a real live blush before. It strikes me as different.

'How different?' she asked, 'doesn't everyone blush?'

Nowadays girls don't think they're supposed to blush. You know, I show my line of bras to a woman buyer. I tell her how they fit, how the cups hold and mold the figure, how the padded ones give a girl something she hasn't got, so she can go out and fool ' he stopped short 'there you go blushing again.'

Francie toyed with the spoon in her cup. It was a moment before she could look at him again. 'I'm sorry.'

'Don't be sorry. I'm tired of having every smart female I meet try to convince me how much cleverer they are than I am. Maybe they are, maybe not. But dammit, .does it always have to be a game with them?'

Francie looked him right in the eye, 'I never had the chance to play games with a bigcity man.' Then realising how serious she sounded she started to laugh. George]omed

After a while she suggested that he visit her at the farm. It seemed only natural to invite him. He had bought her cake and coffee. She told him how to get out there and he said he would come the following night.

When she got home she told her father to be polite when George arrived.

George did come the following night. He brought a small package he gave to her secretly, telling her that he had guessed the size and to open it in her room when she was alone She guessed correctly what was in the package. Her father was polite and George left, not late, after first telling her he would be back on the weekend. She couldn't wait to rush into the room, try on the transparent, bra with the lace trim and pose in front of the mercurystained mirror. Then she noticed that the bra was padded and she wondered how George had been able to tell that she usually did wear padded bras. All alone in the room she laughed aloud, not because of the bra but because it was easy to deal with a 'bigcity' man.

'No girl that age could be a virgin,' a friend of George s told him.

But still George was not convinced. After all, she was forever blushing.

He returned on the weekend. Francie played the piano, touched his hand lightly for a moment when she served dinner. They sat outside until dark. Her father came out, coughed, and George got up to go, promising he'd be back in about a week or ten days.

'My girl is positively pure,' he tried to convince a friend, 'She's not like these broads you hole up with.'

'Bull!' his friend was unconvinced, 'she's like any other chick. Only it will take you a little longer to lay this one.'

'You don't understand/ George whined.

George called his home office and told them he needed more time to cover the territory. Francie had become a mild

Obsession. He wanted to believe that she had remained a virgin all her life; and he also wanted to find out what it meant to sleep with such a girl. He didn't want to hurt her; he couldn't think of treating her as he had a dozen other girls. In point of fact. he was beginning to more than just like her.

They had known each other for more than a month.

Francie's father no longer came out and coughed a reminder for George to leave. They were sitting on. the hammock when Francie suggested they go for a walk. They sat down at the edge of the barn, leaning against each other. In a moment George had turned Francie's face to his and kissed her lightly on the lips, then hugged her hard.

'George. George.' Francie whispered. She pressed her breasts against him, stretching so that the loosely buttoned blouse intentionally opened. She wanted him to touch her all over. She patted his head, felt the side of his face. George started to pull back but Francie pulled him closer.

George touched her thighs, then higher, and she spread her legs inviting him to come to her.

He hesitated, wondering briefly whether all women knew what to do without training, without prior knowledge, or whether his friend had been right about Francie.

'Don't you want me, George?' she asked softly.

'I want you, yes; he told her.

'Then now, George; she took his hand and placed it against her breast. In the darkness she had removed her bra. She put her other hand on his lap. They remained in that position for a moment. George made a feeble attempt to move away.

'Don't leave me now; she pleaded, _ _

He didn't want to spoil her. But her warm feminine scent overpowered him. He dug his hands into her firm bottom pushed her dose, ground her body against his, moving and twisting it till they meshed, one churning into the other digging for gold beneath the surface, then striking home. bursting upward into heaven...

Spent, exhausted, they clung to each other. There was a feelmg of guilt and joy, intermixed. He wanted to say someLg and it was. Will you marry me?' He notoriy wanted to ask her but felt he must not leave her now. His virgin.

George8 started to apologise for having let himself be carried away sexually, but she shushed him. They got up and went in to join "her father.

Later that evening, after George had left and h^tefor the wedding had been set, Francie and her father were settling down for the night.

'Well I did it. Poppa,' she told him.

'You sure did, Francie,' he answered with a laugh.

'I got a father for that baby I'm having by that soldierboy who passed through here last month.'

Chapter Four

THE FRIGID WOMAN GAME

Mae D., we'll call her, had been raised in a strict fundamentalist family tradition, typical of much of the deep South. Yet, living in Atlanta, she had a chance to be part of a metropolitan city life, date, and meet a young school teacher.

Mae was personable, attractive, a good conversationalist, the perfect match for Howie who would some day be principal of the school. Although their premarital dating was innocent, the curves of Mae's body, the promise of her looks implied that the marriage would be passionately fulfilled.

The first night was a struggle for Howie. First there was She awkward posing and posturing before getting into the bed, the shyness of dressing and undressing separately, then coming out of the bathroom to already find her in bed, the sheets pulled up to her chin.

Mae had no clothes on. Howie got in beside her, not sure of what he should do, Mae knew what had to be done but not how to get started.

They were awkward, the two of them. He clumsily reached for her, found his mouth on herbreast, then pulled away. She felt his fleshy and hairy body against her, started to pull away then remembered she was married now, and wanted to begin by being a good wife. She allowed him to come to her. She moaned and scratched him, dug her fingers into his back, gave every sign that everything he did pleased her, that the pain was joy, and the joy was fulfillment.

She made him feel like a man. But inside she hurt and the ache made her want to run away. Each night of their honeymoon she gave him every sign that what he was doing was the greatest for the two of them.

In their own apartment he expected the pleasure of the honeymoon to continue. Each night became dreaded, each time he said that he was ready for bed Mae began to think of excuses. Her head ached. Or her back ached, or she was just too tired. But when she thought she might lose him she went to bed with her husband.

Caught between the drive to hold her husband and the fear of every sexual act between them, Mae found herself playing a game that might make her lose her sanity. She was driven to the most farfetched excuses to be away from him, without making him realise what she was doing. She couldn't explain that cold feeling that overwhelmed her, the abject disgust at the sex act. She didn't want her husband to think her abnormal. She loved him and didn't want to lose him.

She learned to cry and tear at him, reach for him, play with him, breathe and exhort him to go on, all the time her body wanted to run, her insides wanted to retch, and her voice wanted to cry out.

Mae started to wear lessattractive clothes, to make herself less appealing. But her reserved school teacher was a man , at home, a man moved by the sight of his wife.

Earlier, another woman had experienced a similar situa ' tion and had written about it most explicitly, H. R. Hays in The Dangerous Sex quotes the famous female writer who wrote under a man's name, George Sand. The Frenchwoman insisted that a woman had a right to her sexuality, and a right to change her partner if she could not find love. She decribed one night: 'When he was fulfilled, satisfied, sated, I lay there motionless beside him. It seemed to me that I could feel the agitation of physical passion, a momentary imperative of bodily desire ... I fought against these lying urgencies of my suffering, knowing full well that it was not in his power to calm them.'

Hays suggests that, although Sand was passionate, she never achieved an orgasm; Mae experienced the same feelings of agitation. However her strict upbringing cast away any thoughts about changing partners. Since that was out of the question, the attempt to preserve the marriage must be made by her.

As the weeks and months went by Howie took to lingering at work, sometimes not coming home until late at night. Going to bed with him became a frightening chore for Mae. Still, without professional consultation, without the benefit of psychiatrists or counselors, she knew she had better change her attitude toward her husband.

She was determined that he would never know how she detested his lovemaking. She sensed that that last shiver of excitement was what it was all about. She would shiver with excitement, too. If she could keep him feeling satisfied that was one thing, but he couldn't really prove he was a man unless he satisfied her.

As the weeks passed the frigid feeling made itself more and more evident, Mae knew she should get help. But she feared that going to a marriage counselor or a psychiatrist would be to admit mental incapacity. She cherished two hopes. One to satisfy Howie enough and two, to keep him from finding another woman.

She took to pretendsleep before he got ready for bed. She tried to hide her body as much as possible. One night Howie was sitting at the supper table, not saying much, drumming the table with his fingers. Mae sensed that Howie was staring at her back while she washed the dishes. Without turning around she asked, 'Something's bothering you?'

Howie was quiet awhile, then answered slowly, "I thought we were going to be happy together, but now I don't know. Everything's different, like the whole marriage is collapsing right here and now. I still love you. But something is wrong and I don't know what it is.'

She knew and knew that he did, too. Mae put down the dishes, wiped her hands dry on the side of her skirt and came over to her husband. She placed a hand on his face. How desperately she wanted to keep him. But how the simplest thing, like touching his face, made her recoil because she knew what it must lead to. 'Don't I make you feel like a man?' She struggled to get the words out.

Howie put his hands on her shoulders, pressed them tightly, 'It's just that all I want to do is rip the clothes off you. I want to fling you on the bed and make you scream, like you used to.'

'Do you want to hurt me?'

'No, I don't want to hurt you, Mae. I just don't want it to be a game. I'm not accusing you of playing a game. I know it's been difficult with everything you have to do.'

She sighed with relief. He mistook it for an invitation. Mae realised that and continued, 'Why don't you try now?' She whispered out the words, hoping he would say no, but knowing full well he wouldn't.

He laughed and told her it was still daylight.

She motioned for him to follow her. The crisis within was reaching a pitch of frenzy. She was afraid of going to bed with him and fearful that she would lose him if she didn't. She suddenly sobbed and went running into the bedroom, flung herself over the bed. Howie followed after her, not knowing why she was sobbing, except that perhaps it was just because she was a woman. She reached out and hung on, not wanting to lose him. He kissed her tearstained face. She pushed him away and got up.

'I'll be all right.'

'Are you sure?'

It wasn't all that dark. Howie saw his wife step out of her dress, her panties fall to the floor while she remained standing, her firm body catching the shadows, her wellformed breasts issuing mounds of welcome. The calves of her legs rippled as Mae tensed forward....

Howie lusted after his wife as he had never lusted before. He saw that she belonged to him and to no one else. He carried her to the bed.

Mae experienced his hands. They seemed cold to her. She felt him chipping away, straining to infuse her with lust. She arched her back as she thought she should. She shivered. She whispered, 'Don't go away, don't go away.' She twisted her body and lied that she wanted him to stay long after he had found satisfaction. Howie, exhausted, asked her if she had had enough.

'Yes, dear,' she said, and let him go.

She improved her play acting day by day. She feared Howie's return from school, yet fought the desire to run away. She forced herself to play with Howie at supper and afterward. She interfered with his work. He put off correcting papers.

'I may flunk my students,' he laughed, 'but you're going to get an A.' ' Mae attempted to laugh back. But it was a false, phony laugh. She fought the idea of one more session in bed . . . though she had inflamed his desires, she ran out of the house.

Three hours later she came back. She told Howie she had been to a movie. In truth, however, she had been to a girl friend, confided her fears and after swearing the friend to secrecy agreed to visit a psychiatrist.

Howie chose to believe his wife... Mae visited her doctor. When Howie asked her where all the money was going, she lied. She wasn't used to lying, and felt he knew, Howie didn't think she was being unfaithful. But he couldn't quite explain her behaviour.

He still had sex with her, but it was more tempered, more even, less rough and wearing on her mind and body.

Without realising it he was contributing to Mae's release from sexual frigidity. Gradually and with the help of a psychiatrist, she was able to conquer her fear and bit by bit to respond to Howie's nowgentle lovemaking.

Some girls like Mae suffer from sexual frigidity bome of ignorance, fundamental values, an inability or lack of desire to articulate their fears. Mae had a basic desire to hold on to her husband which caused her to pretend to like the sex act. Yet the day came when she did feel genuine passion, when she could be moved by him and quiver in genuine pleasure and be fully gratified. Without help she might very well have thought playing The Frigid Woman Game was how mar riage was meant to be. Cora D. had other problems. But she tried to solve them in a similar way. She tried to cover up her fear of sex. Cora was a stately looking girl with a trim figure, taking to wearing tailored clothes which nevertheless cast no doubt as to her femininity. Cora had a passion for the theatre, a morethanpassable voice, some dramatic talent.

She joined an offBroadway threatre company in New York City. In her own small crowd she became something of a sex symbol. She was never in the big time, occasionally made the columns as having been seen in the company of some upandcoming actor or director. She earned her living as a sales girl.

Cora roomed with a young woman who worked as a buyer in a downtown department store and who also had dramatic talent. She was willing to vicariously share Cora's reputation for glamor. She basked, in Cora's little triumphs, her reputation as the poor man's 'courtesan'.

They both laughed at this. They got along well even when

Cora was signed to do a small part in a locally produced motion picture.

She did well enough and was asked to go to Hollywood to make another film. Cora was still really a nobody, but a sexy looking nobody. It was decided to build her up as the new 'sex' goddess. A studio press agent thought to match her up with a young, virile newcomer. Handsome Ron R., making his first film, fit the bill. Cora imagined that their dates would be for the convenience of columnists. On the other hand Ron thought of Cora as a very desirable woman.

They made a striking couple. Cora managed to keep Ron at arm's length. The press ran reports about their going out together. The fan magazines spoke of their forth coming marriage. Imagination mothered the act. Cora began to feel that perhaps it might be a good idea to marry Ron. After all, he was surely going to command a fine salary m years to come. And Cora wanted to quash a certain ugly rumor concerning her that occasionally cropped up.

Still she dreaded the day they would be married. He couldn't believe that she meant to stay away from him until the wedding night.

They had come back to her apartment after a local movie premiere They had answered the usual inane questions and admitted that marriage was m the offing. The master ot ceremonies gushed at his 'exclusive'.

She flopped into a chair, spread her legs out in front of her, and lay limp. 'What an idiot he was,' she told Ron. Get me a drink, hon?'

She wondered, while he went for the drmk, whether to tell him what kind of a marriage to expect. But she thought better of it. When he came back she motioned for him to sit at her feet.

'You know Ron, dear,' she stroked bis head, marriage will be good for both of us.'

Ron reached up and touched her leg. She felt nothing, but didn't want him to know that. She smiled and he took it as a signal to begin lovemaking. First he was gentle, rising to kiss her on the face, the side of the neck, allowing his hand to reach under and caress her bosom. As a woman, she felt nothing as an actress, everything.

When he carried her into the bedroom she recoiled. There was every chance, she imagined, of ruining her future and messing up a career. Supposing she got pregnant? That would really do her in.

Ron caressed her into submission. She didn't know what to do. She sensed that it was all wrong, that she shouldn't just lie there and let him handle her.

The Frenchman Robert deBlois had long ago advised lady readers in published Love Guides (as reported by Nina Epton in her book. Love and the French), 'Do not let a man put his hand upon your breast, except he who has the right too, because there is always a danger of his becoming so overheated by such maneuvers as to claim the "surplus". For the same reason, never let a man touch your lips, kisses attract other things. And do not wear your dresses cut too low....'

Those words had been written seven hundred years before. but without having read them Cora knew their truth. She had, for reasons of her own, offered herself to Ron. Now he could not stop.

Deliberately, with intent to deceive for her own gain, Cora (like Mae) covered her contempt for sex with a man with glowing gushings of gratification.

Ron didn't know, let alone guess, that each movement Cora made when they were in bed together was an act. Nevertheless, no matter how much she acted, no matter how much she moaned and clutched the sides of the bed as Ron dug into her; no matter how many times she whimpered as if in pleasure, no matter how much she hissed through clenched teeth that he was doing fine she resented his lovemaking. When he was through,spent and asleep beside her, she spent the rest of the night feeling sorry for herself.

Cora's fame grew when the picture was released. The film itself had been panned by the critics. Her personal notices were good. The producers, in order to bolster attendance, sent her on a publicity tour. The first stop was New York.

The moment she was free Cora rang up her former roommate. She took a cab to their old apartment. Her friend of earlier times yawned a sleepy hello.

'Didn't you miss me?' Cora asked.

'Yes, I did,' her roommate answered.

Cora didn't wait another word. She stretched herself out on the bed. 'I'm tired, exhausted. I miss this place. I was happy here.'

'You have everything,' the girl pointed out.

'Not quite,' Cora said and patted the bed.

In moments they were in each other's arms, the con queror and the conquered. They swarmed over each other, finding real pleasure. Cora writhed in true response, real exultation, so strong that she frightened her lover, actually frightened her....

'Are you coming back?'

'You don't understand,' Cora went on. 'There's Ron ... he doesn't know....'

'My God!' the roommate shouted, 'You mean that idiot doesn't know the score?'

'He's not an idiot. Well, maybe he is kind of simple. But he's an awfully good actor.'

'Okay, okay. But what kind of man is he? Can't he tell?'

'No,' Cora smiled. 'When we go to bed he thinks I'm the right partner. But he scares me. Sometimes I find myself with a lump in my throat. It's the damnedest thing. But then we get started and you'd think I'd been playing the part all my life. He thinks I'm the best thing that ever happened to him in bed. But I need you, dear. This is no act.'

'Are you sure, Cora?'

'What do you mean, am I sure? Of course, I'm sure.'

'You might be acting with me, not even knowing that you're acting.'

'Don't be silly, sweetheart, don't be foolish. This is the real thing,' Cora said almost crying. 'Of course Ron hasn't changed my feelings for you.'

The girl hesitated, then held out her arms to Cora.

'Then take me back with you to Hollywood.'

'I I can't,' Cora said, 'it would look funny.'

'No it wouldn't, you know that. Please, Cora?'

'On second thought,' Cora said, 'maybe it would be a great idea.'

'Just don't be cold with me.'

'I won't.' Cora kissed the girl. 'Ron will tell you I'm no frigid wife.'

As Hollywood marriages go, Ron and Cora had a long run, twentytwo months. Throughout, if Ron suspected Cora was playing a game. he never let on. They parted the best of friends.

Cora remarried two months after the divorce became final. This time a producer who could further her career. He, too, did not suspect Cora's homosexual proclivities.

Ron never suspected that Cora had played The Frigid Wife Game. That is, until he read in the paper that Cora's second husband was suing for divorce and had named as corespondent the roommate she had brought west from New York.

Finally, for Cora, the game was over.

Mae was from the mountain country; Cora was 'in*. They both, for reasons of their own, needed a cover for the fear of sex with a man brought on.

With them the fear was genuine. But there is another type of girl, usually found in college, who plays The Professional Virgin Game.

Chapter Five

THE PROFESSIONAL VIRGIN GAME

There's a type of girl, most often found in college, who parades her chastity as a badge of honor. Of course, there are married women, too, even after they have children who pretend they don't know what caused their pregnancy.

In some rare cases a woman will profess virginity to the very end. A widow in her seventies bemoaned the fact that she had never had children. When a young, sympathetic neighbor asked whether she or her husband had been sterile, the old woman answered neither. Pressed further for an explanation the old lady said simply that they never had children because they had never engaged in intercourse. She was afraid the neighbors would think her dirty.

Absurd, you think, that a woman could carry this attitude with her all through life? Look at the women who giggle at a sensual love scene in the movies, who titter nervously at a dirty joke, who anxiously pull down their skirt over their knees, recoil at a strange man's touch.

On occasion inhibition is real; but more often than not it is superficial. It is a carefully nurtured production, applied as meticulously as mascara and perfume.

A coed plays The Professional Virgin Game with the added advantages of education and either real or professed intellectuality. She scores with each new conquest who thinks she has been exclusively his. She can hide her brain behind coquetry. As Brigid Brophy wrote in the Saturday Evening Post a woman 'is inclined to think that intelligence would be as unbecoming to her as a moustache; and ... many women have tried ... to disembarrass themselves of intelligence as though it were false hair.'

Nancy S. was just such a girl. A junior in a small southern college she had the attitude of someone always 'fifteen going on sixteen'. That is she wanted to appear an innocent teenager forever. Nancy was no more than five feet tall, amply proportioned, with bright blue eyes and naturally blonde hair.

Her wish to appear innocent in college stemmed from promiscuous high school days. She was the girl the guys had whispered about. Nancy was the date everyone had made. She played with sex as a kid does a toy. She had sex with almost every boy she knew. There was nothing unloving about her. She didn't have much finesse. She knew how to get right to the heart of the matter. She took a special delight in finding an innocent youngster, maybe a year or so younger than she, but old enough to beg for her body. She never made them wait long. She was short on discretion but long on spirit. She knew what kind of a reputation she had and didn't really care. No one was going to make sport of her to her face, not when that seductive body was waiting to be had

However, when she went away to college, the change of scenery caused her to grow up, even if it didn't diminish her sex desire. She wanted more than a teen fling, she wanted something permanent. And the one way to do that was to be what she wasn't, a professional virgin.

She was a cheerleader, kicking her legs high so that her lace underpants showed, then coyly dropping to her knees so that her skirt covered her legs. That was how she acted off the field, too. Inviting, but never giving.

Unlike the girl who wanted to parade her innocence until the wedding night. Nancy wanted to be a virgin, only m the mind of the particular boy she was dating. She knew that any tales of past promiscuity would go unbelieved by the current boy friend, simply because he did not want to acknowledge them.

Nancy's victory in The Professional Virgin Game could only be achieved when she had landed the man who could give the security she wanted. All earlier conquests were considered minor skirmishes. She was determined not to win the battle and lose the war. Therefore she played each fellow as if he were the last.

There would be no complications as long as each boy she dated knew the rules of the game. Where she ran into trouble was Pete who, at the age of twenty, was one hundred per cent chaste and just barely kissed.

As each female brings her own rules of behavior to

each game she plays, so does each man. In this case Pete was attracted to Nancy by her lace panties, a fact which he would deny even to himself. His outward reason was her mind, the grades she got in school. Nancy could not hide her academic prowess.

Pete became Nancy's goal because his family was loaded and Pete was the heir apparent.

None of Pete's fraternity brothers had the heart to tell him that Nancy was a fake.

One said. 'It will be good for him. He needs to get his feet wet. He'll find out for himself.'

Another. 'She's a goddamn screwing machine'. But no one could lay actual claim or offer proof.

Pete overheard their conversations, he never let on he knew they were referring to him and Nancy. Instead he took her for walks in the park; they studied together and after three weeks he shyly held her hand.

'I think you're very nice,' she told him one warm after noon as they sat on the grass, studying for an exam.

She leaned closer to him so that he could see an unbrassiered round warm breast. He pretended not to see. But he did and she knew it.

Pete fought what stirred inside him and turned his attention to the exam they were preparing for.

'Why don't you come over to my room tonight? My roommate has to be away and it will be quiet. We can study together.' There was such an innocence, an utter simplicity about her, that Pete could only think she genuinely wanted to study. There was nothing in his experience to suspect anything else.

Nancy, who had kept this pretense of sweetness and innocence far longer than she wanted, would have preferred to grab him, hang on, and make him scream with pleasure. She wanted to curse and swear and possess him with all her body. But to do that would blow the game. She had tried with others and found they had nothing more permanent to offer than an expression of lust.

As with so many women who play games at all, she was caught between immediate desire and longrange goals. Nancy wanted to be sure that Pete didn't just think of her as a sex machine. When he 'won' her, she wanted him to think that it was the first time for her.

In her quiet times alone Nancy thought of herself as the woman described by Dr Renatus Hartogs in Four Letter Word Games: 'Obscene selfdescription is fairly common among women with sexual conflicts or uncertainties. Women who, for whatever reasons, find it difficult to form satisfactory love relationships sometimes try to assert their sexuality through obscene talk. Typically such women believe that men do not think of them as persons but merely as "cunts".'

They were to study for their biology exam. Nancy asked Pete what gonads were. She knew of course. He blushed and told her.

'There,' she patted him, as if accidentally. He jumped back, stopped by the edge of the couch.

Pete put down the book. He wanted to do something. He wanted to tell her how he felt. But he couldn't articulate, express the emotion he felt overwhelming him.

Nancy strained at her passionate leash. She wanted to hold Pete, and have him dig his fingers into her. But to approach him openly would give everything away. Instead she whispered softly, close to his ear. The vibrations she set up sent shivers throughout his body. The top of her tongue, snakelike, flicked into his ears. He suffered a pleasurable. unidentifiable anguish.

'I read someplace,' she told him, 'that a woman knows when she wants a. man.' She let the words sink in, pausing long enough for him to know exactly what she meant. 'I mean a girl just knows when the right man comes along. I've been so afraid that the first man I gave myself to would be the wrong one.' Nancy spoke haltingly as if every word came out with great effort. She made the sentence sound like a confessional. Pete didn't answer. She took his hand and put it in her lap, sensing that his fingers wanted to probe, to grope and find what delights were there. She turned and the edge of her bosom brushed his chest.

'I can't imagine this happening to me.'

'I can't either.' Then clumsily, he fumbled for her dress zipper. She helped him loosen it. It never occurred to him that a girl with no experience would act more shyly.

Nancy seemed to answer his every question. She told him, as she pressed her body against his. 'This is the way it should be. This is what should happen. I feel it in my bones, instinctively.'

'But I don't know how...' Pete blustered.

She stopped him with her hand against his mouth.

'We'll find out together, Pete darling. That's the best way.'

'But'

'You'll find the way. But be quick.' She reached for

him. Pete found himself drawn toward her, not at all sure that what he was doing was right, not at all confident of his abilities. He wanted to stay and be part of her but didn't know whether or not he was even in the right spot.

After repeated mishaps, all he could muster was, 'Are you all right. Nancy?'

She gave up, spent, exhausted by her frustrated desire, her playedout passion. The rules of the game were strict. But, could she convince Pete that he was her first man he would be hooked. An announcement of their engagement would ensue.

Right now Nancy had to assuage her own desire, while at the same time convince Pete that she was a novice and get him to propose.

Pete's very own innocence played into her plans, me rules of The Professional Virgin Game are such that, even in the very act, the girl must appear untouched.

Pete lay prone and Nancy moved into place again, twisting beneath him and grimacing. Pete mistook that for pain. He felt an unidentifiable guilt. It rose up and around him. He could only ask. 'Will you marry me?'

She whispered yes, grabbed him around the neck and pressed his flushed face against her. moving his hands over her breasts, tickling his ears, rubbing the side of his neck. whispering encouragement all the while.

They consummated their relationship.

Dressing later, he averted his eyes. He, too, seemed embarrassed. They announced their engagement. All this would have made a fine ending. Except for a few things. Pete's buddies now tried to warn him away. He didn't believe what they told him about her.

Nancy and Pete were engaged until the end of the semester. Forced to live a discreet, careful life. Nancy soon grew bored with Pete, who was genuinely innocent. Main taining the rules of The Professional Virgin Game became

more than she could bear. There was only one thing to do, break the engagement. When a girl plays The Professional Virgin Game she may let herself in for unheralded and unexpected complications. Hays in The Dangerous Sex quotes a French Bishop, Marbod de Rennes, who maintained that women came between old friends, separated lovers, set children against their elders, destroyed villages, cities and whole people. A Benedictine monk, Bernard de Moraix, was convinced there are no good women on earth. Others held that intercourse only served to shorten a man's life.

What these learned gentlemen made no note of, was what happens when a girl playing The Professional Virgin Game comes between a young man and his mother.

Janet L. had set her eyes on a classmate. They were both freshmen. She had come to this northern New England col lege from New York City. Her parents had insisted she go to this small school, to keep away from the temptations of the big city Janet was eighteen and touched by every eligible male on the high school football team. She had blossomed and burgeoned with sex. She was tall, nearly five feet nine with long black hair. dark eyes, nearwhite skin that con trasted sensuously with her hair and eyes. She affected little girl clothes. It appeared as if they were made too small or she had outgrown them. However, they served to show off her legs and hips and bosom.

It was a small, proper school, not given to demonstrations or illicit fun. She wasn't allowed to smoke nor was there alcohol available. She was a fair student but found no chal lenge in the classroom. For the most part the boys were 'square' or worse, not interested in girls.

Because she was attending this college against her own desires she started off slowly, socially that is. Usually Janet came on strong.. fended passes with knowledgeable tech.

niques, gave in on her terms and otherwise played The Smart Girl Game.

Instead, at this school, Janet was subdued, nearly sullen. The other girls and young men mistook this mood for shyness. Janet found herself receiving another type of attention which, she reasoned, was due to the new posture she was assuming. She found it especially interesting that boys regarded her as an innocent. If she made an indelicate comment they thought she was daring. And so, quite naturally, Janet played her part and fell into The Professional Virgin Game.

What disturbed her was the purpose to which she could put this game. The game is played without formalising the rules. There was no single outlet or direction until she met Len. He was a gangling six footer from the northern part of the state. In his own rugged and taciturn way he was hand some and attractive. She didn't appear to excite or other wise interest him. She made every meeting serve to identify her pride in virtue. It was more than innocence; this virginity was something to be worn with distinction as a football player wears his letter, a graduate displays his degree, a banker his notes.

Janet hinted she'd like to be invited to the weekend dance.

'I'd like to take you to the dance,' Len said in his slow deliberate way, 'but my mother is coming to visit me and I have to spend the time with her.'

Every approach she made was thwarted by mention of his mother. When she suggested that perhaps his mother might not care, he became indignant and Janet feared he would leave her standing there. 'I have to spend the time with mother. I had no father. I mean, mine died when I was born. I'm everything to my mother,' he explained.

Janet tried another tack, 'Well, maybe your mother would like to be with us.' If she couldn't fight them, maybe she could join them.

Len was not anxious to let his mother know of this suggestion. However, reluctantly, he agreed.

'But, mother,' he told her when she got into town, 'Janet is a nice girl, a very nice girl, you'll see.'

Len's mother patted her son on the shoulder; 'I'm sure she is. And someday when you're ready I'll want you to marry a nice girl. But right now, you're not ready to get mixed up with a girl. Mother knows.'

When Janet learned Len's mother had said no, she made up her mind to meet her. She called her on the telephone, introduced herself on a pretext and asked to show her around town.

Janet played the simple girl, took every occasion to let Len's mother know how proud she was to be chaste, wear ing the very symbol as a badge of honour. It made no difference. Len would not leave his mother.

'Maybe this girl is everything you say, Len. But I doubt it; his mother told him, 'soon she'll take you for your money and mine, too.'

'I can't believe that. It isn't that I don't love you. I do. I love her, too. It's different. You understand.'

Len's mother seized him in her arms. 'Someday, when you're older you'll understand; She kissed him. "Right now I think you still need me;

'I don't know. I'm kind of mixed up. I don't want to leave you alone, of course.'

Len's mother might have told him what Miss Brophy wrote in the Saturday Evening Post when she said, 'The male has accused woman of bewitching him with sex, of destroying him with her organ and her appetite, or of betraying him with a real or imaginary stallionlike rival.

Or he turns upon her and calls her carrion and identifies her with sin or describes her as tiger or a cannibalistic spider.

By using this symbolic magic he has either imprisoned her, made her an outcast, or treated her as a scapegoat'

In a sense, that was the feeling that Len's mother exhibited, the sentiment that Janet inferred when Len told her what his mother had said. At first Janet wanted to go to the woman, tell her she was a hypocrite, only wanted her son for herself, that she was destroying him. Instead she thought of a better plan. She would win Len with her innocence, deprive him of his virtue and. so give him what his mother could not, the animalism, the passion and contempt that could come with sex.

The Professional Virgin Game was ideally suited. Len understood this symbol; it would not throw him off guard, would not cause him to run away. He could be seduced into agreement as he slept with Janet and envisioned his mother on the bed.

Janet reasoned that what Len really wanted to do v/as to sleep with his mother. But customs being what they are he couldn't possibly do this. Yet the subconscious desire to be with this older woman was strong enough to keep him from getting seriously involved with any girl. To Len all women, except his mother, were inherently evil, ready to 'bewitch him with their sex'.

Janet's only hope was to convince Len that she was not only pure, but proudly so, that she could sing hallelujah to virginity with the same zeal he went to church. Then when he was convinced she would throw him on to the bed and glory in the conquest that would not only prove her sexual power but destroy the older woman whom she had come to regard as a rival.

Len's mother admonished her son about girls, especially college girls. He was speaking more and more of this girl who helped him with his studies, walked with him on the campus, visited local museums and was otherwise a paragon of virtue. She decided to call on Janet.

'Why I like Len,' Janet told her, 'there's nothing serious, you should know that.'

'What I really mean,' the older woman told her, 'is that I don't want you to chase after him.'

At this Janet lost her cool. She reacted, 'Why you old fool, you know what? I'm going to have your son and you'll never be able to convince him it was wrong.'

'You wouldn't,' the older woman screamed, but Janet

had turned her back and walked away.

The next day Len told her, 'Janet someone must be telling my mother awful things about you. I wouldn't repeat them.'

Janet told him there was always someone who was jealous and evil. Let it go at that.

'But Len,' she asked, 'would you like to take me to dinner? We could go Dutch if you're broke.'

He agreed, as much to make up for the things he had repeated as just to be with her. She suggested after dinner they walk to her room.

Janet boarded with a family who had gone away for the week. Len sat on the edge of the chair. Janet asked, 'Don't you think much about girls, Len?'

'I guess,' he said.

'I think about boys, I mean I sometimes wonder, that's only natural, Len. Of course, that's all.'

Janet walked out of the room to change her clothes. She came back in a few moments wearing what appeared to be diaphanous, loosefitting pajamas. They were white and longlined, making her a striking, revealing figure. The blossoms of her breasts swelled the fabric, the darkness of the creases of her thighs made shadows on the cloth. She stood in the doorway, knowing the light behind her outlined her limbs, made the flesh come alive.

There was no doubt that Len noticed her, that it was having an effect on him. He moved his legs, tried to cover his excitement, his discomfort. But he said nothing, only stared.

Janet came over and sat beside him, allowing the warmth of her legs to brush against him. She fondled and petted him, kissed him, stuck her tongue in his ear and yet he remained motionless. She reached over and took his hand, placed it on her leg, moved it up so that it caught the firm nipple of a breast. She pushed him down, reaching for his manliness, wanting him to do something, anything. Still he held back.

Janet forgot the letter V she wore emblazoned on her front and back. She moved the challenge to the dare. She massaged his legs, got him to respond slightly, make an effort to be part of what she was doing. She knew. she felt, he was there but wondered if his mother was still coming between them. Slowly he responded as in a trance, began to stroke her thighs. Then with surprising zeal he was on top of her, pushing into her, making her scream, grabbing at. her shoulders, clawing the skin until the blood ran. He fought her to the side of the bed and off it on to the floor, never letting go. She felt a pain inside that she had never felt before, an exultation she had most certainly never expected.

At first Janet kept her eyes closed. When she opened them, she nearly screamed. Len's face was taut, almost maddening in its wild stare, his eyes open, his mouth showing drops of spittle at the comers. He yelled at her to stay where she was.

'You bitch." he screamed, 'you bitch. I'll give you what you want, what you've always wanted. And he proceeded to cut her in half, her body ached from groin to bottom, from shoulder to toe; her head in pain from both fear and pleasure, the maddest combination of sensations.

Then, as quickly as it began, it was over. Len sat by himself, crosslegged on the floor. He was crying. Janet, relieved that it had ended, yet not unhappy that it had happened, heard his faint cries of 'Mother, mother'.

She went over to him, gently rested her head on his shoulder, 'No dear, it's me, Janet

He started to say 'mother' again, then uttered, deliberately, 'Janet, my Janet'.

She got up from the floor, looked at him. He looked up, 'No matter what,' he told her, 'I want you, only you.'

Janet smiled, touched him, then went into the other room to make a phone call. When his mother answered, she said, I just wanted to tell you that I just gave Len something you never could. I'm sure you'll be the first one he tells we re getting married.' She hung up the phone and went back to join Len.

Chapter Six

THE LET'S BE ADULT ABOUT IT GAME

There's no doubt that college experience determines to a great extent the social and sexual behaviour a woman will engage in, in married life. In Sex and the College Student, by the Group for the Advancement of Psychiatry, this point is made, ', . . there is a consensus that the double standard increasingly is being discarded and that college girls more often seek sexual experience during the college years than their mothers did.' In another section it is noted that 'Corn. pulsive sexual activity usually represents an unresolved conflict and an attempt to relieve anxiety rather than simple pursuit of pleasure . . . When sex is used solely to prove power and dominance, sexual expression can veer in patho logical directions.'

At college, Karen R. was everything a coed should be. She was vivacious, more handsome than beautiful, short but perfectly proportioned with long blonde hair that defied detection as to its original color. She was a betterthan average student. Her family was financially comfortable. With all this one would assume she had everything and could be choosy as to whom she dated. But Karen, for reasons that go back to her childhood an indifferent father and a domineering mother suffered, the damning anxieties of insecurity. She so much wanted to be loved that she willingly gave herself to every boy who took her out. Her reputation for promiscuity was so great that she became a freshman's first date, his easy breakingin to sex. She offered herself with the hope that this would be the bond that assured her love and respect. Instead, of course, she became a sex joke on campus, her initials were scrawled by the dorm telephone, and her former dates called impatiently and were often frustrated, the waiting list was solong.

So many dates only abetted her anxiety, her fear of not being wanted. She did whatever a boy wanted and often what he did not expect. When it began to appear she would continue this free life after graduation she met a graduate student. Don was tall and goodlooking; he was physically attractive and had continually made the honor lists but, with all that, was shy with girls and quite unwilling to do anything to promote himself.

Don had been urged to date Karen. His friends thought she might be able to get him out of his social shell. As it turned out he found much in common with Karen, was m tune with her views on life and politics. Sexually he made an adequate partner. While he accepted this part of their relationship as necessary, he was the first man to be intrigued by Karen's good mind. Karen, in turn, immediately became aware that in Don she had found someone who com plemented her own desires for total attention. It was no problem to get him to propose.

Soon Don was offered a position doing research for the college The pay was relatively low. certainly much lower than he could have achieved in private industry. No matter how much Karen insisted he was worth more, Don was quite unwilling to look elsewhere. The womblike security the college afforded was something he had no intention of leaving.

While Karen had no desire to leave Don they were a well balanced twosome she knew there should be more to life than a small college town. If anything, she would have to be the one to promote him. First, she reasoned, get him named head of the department, then to private industry and the big money.

The trouble was Don was not ambitious for himself. He took whatever praise he got for a new discovery as an end in itself. It wasn't until a dance was held at the local country club that Karen had her first opportunity.

Attending the dance was one Mr C., the major donor to the college laboratory in which Don worked. He was in his middle sixties, accompanied by a talkative wife who bullied him about, made unsubtle references to his overweight, reminded him publicly of slight personal failings and otherwise made his life intolerable. Nevertheless Mr C. maintained a good humor. Karen had heard stories about his miserable home life and made it her business to be introduced to him.

Mr C. was a willing dance partner. After the first one he suggested they have a. drink. 'But it's only punch,' Karen told him.

Mr C., keeping a watchful eye on his wife, slapped Karen playfully on the bottom. When Karen didn't protest he went on, 'I have a special bottle in my locker. Why not join me?'

She didn't want to seem too easy. 'I don't know. The party is just beginning. And my husband is alone. I think I should stay with him, don't you?'

'He'll be well taken care of. Do I know your husband?'

'No,' she said taking him by the arm. 'but I'm sure you will.'

They escaped their respective mates.

From that time on it was easy. After a few drinks Mr C. became lovingly amorous. Karen put him off with a 'maybe' that he understood to mean he should try again..

A few days later he was a surprise visitor to her apartment. What he had come for ostensibly was to talk about her husband. Karen turned the gambit to her advantage. She let him rest his hand on her knee, told him how impressed she was with his knowledge of the college research department, and otherwise treated him as his wife did not. Against his protestations she ushered him out, but not before she kissed him on the cheek and said, 'How wonderful it is that the college has a man of such vision working for it.'

Mr C. suggested that he could use her ideas and asked if they couldn't meet for lunch. He named a place and day. Karen agreed. Phase One of The Let's Be Adult About It Game was over.

During lunch Mr C. suggested that it might be a good

idea and be helpful to him at the same time, if Karen would look at and give him her opinion of his college expansion plans. She protested mildly but went with him after lunch.

They were no sooner in the room than he told her how attractive she was, at the same time reminding her how much his wife misunderstood him.

Karen asked, 'What do you think Don's chances for promotion are?'

'Excellent, my dear, excellent,' he said, at the same time rather hesitatingly kissing her on the cheek.

Karen wasn't too anxious; not yet. She wanted to hear more about Don.

'Yes, yes.' Mr C. said impatiently, sweat starting to bead his forehead, 'of course I'll send a recommendation through the first thing tomorrow.'

'This afternoon,' she corrected.

'This afternoon,' he agreed.

Karen was slow with him. The older man puffed and couldn't quite deal with her young animal body. He wasn't able to accomplish much. Karen helped him along, complimenting him tenderly, so that he swelled with pride and accomplishment. He had barely consummated the relationship before Karen was getting dressed.

The next day Don told Karen he was getting a raise and change in title.

'Because you deserve it.' she told him. They spent a pleasant, rewarding night together.

Karen periodically met Mr C. And successively Don's salary was increased. Then one day the old man told Karen that he wanted to leave his wife and marry her.

She was firm in her answer. 'The one thing you forget is that we're adults. I know perfectly well what I'm doing and so do you. I got some of the things I wanted and you got something too. We can be grown up.'

'You mean, this was only to get your husband promoted?' She didn't answer but smiled.

'I could have it work the other way,' he told her.

'But you won't,' she was staying sweetly, 'you won't take a chance on ruining your reputation at the risk of mine, not with your wife. So you go back to her like a good boy.'

The game was over.

It was no problem to get Don to apply to private industry. The taste of higher financial rewards proved too much a lure. And in private industry Karen played the same game. But here she was more careful about whom she played with. She just wanted to be sure she could get out without difficulty. With the exception of one rather outwardly gentle executive who ended up wanting to beat her, and use straps and chains, she didn't get into too much trouble.

When she found out that the man could be gratified by being bathed by her, she complied. What he did succeed in was working her up to a state of such high anticipation that by the time she got home she was ready to tear her husband apart.

At this writing Don is chief research officer for a promi nent pharmaceutical firm. He and his wife are on everyone's social invitation list. They are pillars of their community. There is no doubt that Don does not suspect what his wife has been doing and continues to do, to further his career. Karen has found an outlet for the same type of feeling for sensual pleasure that carried her through college. She makes deliberately sure that each man knows why she is willing to go with him. She is willing to treat him as a prostitute's trick so long as he knows what is expected of him. She lets them know she is an adult, fully aware of what she wants out of life. In her own way she loves her husband, is able to separate her love for him from what she thinks she must do to further his position and hers, too.

As the chairman of the board or Don's present firm told Karen one night, 'you're so damn cold and warm at the same time.' They were quite nude and motionless on the hotel room bed. He had made vain attempts to clutch her and she had pushed him away. It wasn't until he promised to authorise a European business tour for Don and herself that she allowed him to touch her.

The coldness vanished. There was desire where there had been indifference; there was a smile where there had been displeasure. The chairman of the board clumsily reached for her.

'For a man who knows so much,* she told him, 'you know nothing.' She placed his hand where his fingers did the walking, down the welltraveled road. She excited and agitated him, she outvoted his protests, made him the one hundred per cent stockholder of her person, twisting and turning, giving him no option but to continue, restraining him, then holding back, and in one loud acclamation, elect ing him to the highest office.

Tired, exhausted he lay back, attempting feebly to hold her beside him. But Karen was up and dressing. 'Tomorrow is another day, another promotion. Don't be childish. We can both be adult about what we want.'

The chairman of the board understood. He sighed. 'Of course.'

Karen played The Let's Be Adult About It Game with the finesse and success of a professional which she was. It has been said that middleaged women are capable of giving a man the greatest sexual pleasure. They are, generally, more capable of dispensing with superficial inhibitions, especially if they have lived a full and complete life. This type of woman more easily relaxes in the presence of men, is able to establish an easy communication. It is this woman, too, who can play her version of The Let's Be Adult About It Game with a mature directness.

As with every game we have discussed this one leads to a man's entrapment. The motivation may vary from biological necessity to power and prestige. While it is true that when most men desire a woman, they will settle for any woman, the opposite does not always hold true. The exception is that time of month when a woman comes closest to a man in her desire for sex.

Too many women, inhibited by their family upbringing, their church, their environment, will not admit this last fact, even to themselves. But take Ivy L., fortyseven years old, collegeeducated, married for over twenty years to a hardworking husband who was able to provide her with a good suburban home outside of Chicago, two teenage children and enough money to get an occasional new dress and go out to dinner at least once a week. While this might have satisfied many women it only indicated to Ivy that she could do better. When she looked in the mirror she saw a figure just slightly touched by age, a firm bosom, broad hips, and well-defined thighs and legs. Her facial wrinkles were easily hidden with powder and makeup. The few specks of grey in her dark hair looked as if they had been intentionally put there. All in all, she thought, I still have much to offer a man. And she didn't necessarily mean her husband.

Ivy was at a restless stage of life. She affected skirts that might have been thought too younglooking, but she knew she had good legs. She was still excited by a strange man's compliments and fantasised what it would be like to go to

bed with someone besides her husband. Her upbringing, experience and style of living kept them only dreams.

It happened one afternoon she found herself shopping on State Street. She had argued that morning with Harold about buying new furniture. She blamed him for not wanting to improve the house. All in all it had been a verbal dragdown brawl. She felt miserable and decided the only thing that would make her feel better was to look for furniture anyway.

The store salesman made a sympathetic audience. Actually Ivy's purchase was secondary to finding someone to listen to her. Subconsciously she was looking for someone sympathetic. When the salesman alluded to her good looks and made complimentary remarks about her figure she was nattered and repelled at the same time. She ended up ordering the furniture.

That evening, when she met Harold, she wore a charmingly seductive negligee, something she hadn't used in years. She had martinis waiting. Harold was surprised.

After dinner Ivy asked, as she sat on the edge of his arm chair, 'Are you tired, dear?'

'It's been a rough day. I am,' he told her.

'But are you too tired, dear?' she asked more emphatically, leaning over so he could see she had nothing on underneath, as if there had been any doubt.

Harold, tired though he was, was only too willing to cooperate. Later, lying in bed, having experienced more pleasure, quick though it was, than he could recall having had for.years, he was ready to agree to almost anything.

'We can manage the new furniture.'

'Great; she told him.

From then on Ivy's life totally changed, its pace became fast and furious. What happened can best be explained by the story she told her attorney eight months later.

She had come into his office feeling distressed, unhappy about what she had to do, but feeling more like a woman than ever before in her life. She was made to feel comfortable and relaxed with a drink. What the lawyer knew he was going to hear would only be a variation on a theme told to him by dozens of other Ivys.

'You see,' she started, 'it seems strange that anyone could be married as long as I have and want a divorce. It all began when Harold agreed to take me with him to his next sales convention. What he didn't know was that I had decided that I would be the glamour wife. I wanted to be taken along so I could prove to him that I was an asset in his business; that I could make his bosses and his customers want me along. I knew that would help Harold. Well, it certainly did.'

She sipped her drink and continued, "The first trip was to Detroit. I remember we went for a drink in a bar just back of the bus station on Woodward, kind of a nice place.

Harold was with. an important customer and I think he was genuinely pleased to have me along. The customer even suggested that Harold work out the details with his assistant and he'd take me back to the hotel where we'd wait for them. It seemed great. Harold was getting an unusually large order. I could tell by the pleased look on his face. Anyway, we went back to the hotel, had a few drinks. The customer, he was about my age, maybe a few years younger actually, he was a good ten years younger he flattered my ego all right. He suggested we wait upstairs in his room. I suppose I had had too much to drink, but I agreed. After all, I was a big girl. He told me that. We weren't in his room more than five minutes when he made love to me.' Ivy put down her drink. The lawyer waited until her momentary embarrassment had passed. 'I suppose I rationalised,' she went on, 'that this was certainly going to help Harold. Our lovemaking was quick though and unsatisfying. I was nervous and he just got me started, before it was all over.'

The lawyer told Ivy she didn't have to go on.

'Oh, but I must,' she insisted relishing the therapeutic quality of her storytelling. 'Harold came back and got me. He didn't suspect anything. In fact he told me that his customer said on the next sales trip Harold should be sure to bring me along. He was quite pleased. But I'll tell you I was nervous and anxious for fear of Harold finding out.'

Ivy became less aware that she was talking to someone. The free thought just flowed. She was able to pick up her story without hesitation.

'Needless to say I went with Harold on almost every one of his trips. His business increased. He got promoted to district manager within three months. You know, he didn't really associate me with the new income. Well. he sort of regarded me as a goodluck charm. I didn't even think of it as being unfaithful. It just seemed that it was an adult thing to do.

'I can remember one youag buyer. He was barely out of his twenties. But he was a man.' Ivy's eyes brightened with fond remembrance. She allowed her cigarette to be lit and continued. 'He was a young man but with an awful lot of influence. I found out later his father was the big man, one of Harold's most influential customers. Oh, but he made me feel like a young girl. I almost laughed when he suggested we go for a drink. By this time it was after two months of traveling, and I was used to all the symptoms. He cried, you know, when we were in bed together. I felt like his mother but I didn't want to tell him. Maybe there is some psycho logical truth to that. I don't really understand all the reasons. But he was so gentle, laying his head against my breast." Ivy was completely uninhibited in her description of what had transpired. 'He kissed me so gently her and there.

I remember him kissing me, slowly, as if he were sucking on both my lips, making me feel with his tongue as if he were inside me.'As young as he was, he was a man. He was the first one to make me feel gratified so soon, so many times.

Even by just kissing me that way, so tenderly but so fully I can still feel the shivers. And later, Harold never suspected. I think that the young man's father did. He made a point of telling me his son had grown up without a mother and he was glad that I was able to spend some time with him and give him the benefit of my maturity. I thought that was pretty funny. After that Harold told me he was glad that I was making such a g6od impression. I remember asking Harold, rather playfully, what he would think if I made such an impression that another man wanted to have an affair . with me. Harold laughed and said it would be great; we both could be adult about it. Of course, he didn't believe it was possible. Anyway it gave me a good excuse to continue behaving and playing a game. That's what it is of course, a game. It's an adult game but it can be dangerous.'

The lawyer nodded an agreement without making any further comment. Ivy, continued. To be honest I was getting more interested in my own pleasure and less in' Harold's business improvement. That was the beginning of the reason why I'm here.'

Ivy seemed spent at this time. She spilled out so much it seemed to take everything out other. She caught her breath and spoke briefly, 'even to this day Harold doesn't know about any of the others.'

The lawyer had to ask why she was in his office, wanting a divorce.

'It's funny,' she began, not at all responsive to his ques tion, 'I've slept with so many men in the last eight months or so. I've had them every way, the beasts and the gentle, the old, so old that they begged me to help them out any way I could. I did, too. I've had them so young they whim pered and cried and some tried to make believe they were big men. All this time I pretended it was something I was doing for Harold, part of a wild game. But, actually, I guess I did enjoy the sex. Well then, Harold got a big promotion to the women's division of his company. All the buyers had been men. But now he was seeing women buyers. There wasn't a thing I. could do to help him. In fact it changed^ Harold had to take them out. You should see those bitches Her voice grew high and angry. 'Some of those frustrated women, cadging for drinks like southside whores. I knew what they were about. Harold was a big man with the company They'd tease him into dinners and drinking all night. I knew what they were up to. But the worst part of it all was that Harold told me he had to entertain them. He didn t spell it out. But I could guess what he was doing. All m the name of getting business. I accused him of sleeping with them. He laughed and told me I had to be an adult. That was part of the selling game. He was making it big, finally. I was getting the financial benefit so I shouldn't complain. I want a divorce because I can't live with him, knowing what he's doing.' She began to cry. .

The lawyer comforted her, told her that perhaps she was being too hasty. Maybe, using some discretion, she could talk with Harold.

That night Ivy told her husband she had been to a lawyer, and why.

If that's the way you feel, dear; he said, I'll get a different position with the firm. I can use a rest. It's been getting to be too much.'

Tor me. too. I guess the game is over, dear.'

'What game?'

She answered, kissing him lingeringly on the side ot the neck. 'The Let's Be Adult Game, of course. That s for kids.'

Chapter Seven

THE MY LIFE IS HELL AT HOME GAME

The poet James Whitcomb Riley described the uses of the word 'hell'. It was a hell of a day when it started to rain, it was a hell of a day when it started to snow, hell when it was hot. In other words hell can be a mighty personal place. Especially so for the wife at home. A kind of particular hell for the middleclass American wife may have been summed up by Eric John Dingwall in. The American Woman when he wrote: 'We have already seen that some of the complaints made by women are that their husbands are absorbed in business, are perpetually tired and are therefore unable to spare the time or take the trouble for the more intimate affairs of the boudoir.'

The undemonstrative husband can, of course, contribute greatly to his wife's feeling of insecurity. Where she otherwise may have had no inclination, inattentiveness can make her search out games to play. She may not realise that part of the responsibility in this incompatible situation lies with her inability to offer him something attractive. This lack of desire to face reality may be more particularly true of American women than European. Yet Jon Whitcomb in All About Girls quotes an American woman friend who was married to a Frenchman. This woman summed up the Frenchwoman's general attitude toward The My Life Is' HellAtHome Game.

According to her, 'In France, the important things in a woman's life are her home, her family and sex, in that order. She will sacrifice the third any day to keep the first two. In cases of extreme incompatibility, she will hang on to the first two, and possibly retrieve the third by taking a lover.'

The middleclass American suburban housewife may disdain the 'taking of a lover'. Her life at home may be hell simply because she hasn't been able to buy clothing or take the trips her neighbors do. Keeping up with the twocar family across the street may put more of a strain on her marriage than her husband's tired body.

As with so many of the games she plays, a woman must give herself a rationale for what she is about to do. In this case it is being deprived of all the good things in life, through 'look what a good wife I've been raising the children cleaning the house, and even going to bed with you once in a while what man could ask for anything more here we are almost povertystricken because you won't take a second job.' There is no punctuation or pause in her sentence. She may say it so often that her husband turns her off with the ease with which he shuts off the television set.

She is out of sight and out of mind.

That is just about the place in which Inez Y. found her self. She lived in a small suburb outside of St. Louis. Clayton had a betterthanaverage cluster of uppermiddleclass housing. Inez's husband was a hardworking sales manager who managed to pay off yesterday's bills with today's salary. This kept him just one jump ahead but inhibited many of the extras Inez would like. He worked hard and long hours, found himself attracted to bis wife, who main tained her youthful figure and looks into her late thirties. Their two small children were never a burden. In fact they were usually asleep when he arrived home. He played it straight. When he said he had to work weekends, that's exactly what he did. Although Inez had no proof to the contrary she had doubts, based on the one fact that he was a man. Inez stewed and spent more than she should as a sort of

revenge for her husband's inattention. While the poor slob broke his back getting enough money for the mortgage and an occasional dinner out, Inez tried desperately to think of some way to break the pattern. She felt putupon and otherwise mistreated, a necessary prerequisite for playing The My Life Is Hell At Home Game.

Finally, Inez happened to talk to a casual acquaintance while sitting under the hair dryer in the beauty shop she ritually attended once a week. The other woman was about ten years older than Inez, a fact she willingly admitted, mostly because she looked much younger and knew it. This particular day Inez was feeling extra putupon. Her husband had refused to take her to a show she wanted to see, had made her return a dress she had just purchased, and had spent the preceding night sleeping alone in the den.

After their hair was dried the two women decided to have lunch together.

'Please call me Ronnie, Veronica sounds almost saintlike and, heaven knows, I'm anything but a saint.' She gave a small chuckle and continued, I know just how you feel, dear, I mean my first husband was like that, my second too. It seems if I married another dozen times they'd all be the same. I guess there must be something true about always ending up making the same mistake.'

"But I love my husband,' Inez said guiltily and almost too quickly.

Romlie patted her hand. 'Have a martini. It's good for the soul, best damn tranquilizer.' She didn't wait for an answer but ordered two from the waiter. 'It's just that there isn't enough money to go around. It's not new.'

Ronnie let Inez admit to that fact. They talked for a while about how difficult it was to do what she wanted, even to get a new dress. Ronnie carried the conversation through more martinis.

The children will be home from school, I must leave,' Inez suddenly remembered.

'I'll drive you home,' Ronnie told her, 'but before we go, would you like to have enough money I mean for the extras you deserve?' She accented the last word.

'Oh, I'd be no good at a job. I can't type, I can't sell. I've thought of it. I just don't know what I could do.'

'Well, I know,' Ronnie spoke softly, 'you come over to my house tomorrow.' She wrote her address on a piece of paper. 'Be there about one. What time do the kids get home from school?'

'Oh, after three.'

'Then be there about noon. I'll tell you all about it.'

Inez agreed.

The next day Inez arrived at Ronnie's home, a large rambling house on the far edge of the town. It was isolated from its nextdoor neighbor by a high hedge.

When Ronnie met Inez at the door, Inez thought it a bit unusual her hostess should be dressed as if for a party. Inside she found a male guest, whom Ronnie introduced as an old friend. Inez hardly remembered his name from the fast, slurred introduction.

When Ronnie, after about fifteen minutes of small talk still hadn't mentioned the job, Inez assumed she was waiting for her other guest to leave. They had a few drinks, although Inez protested it was much too early for her to drink. The liquor felt warm and she had two cocktails, refusing a third.

The man, whose name she still didn't recall, moved over beside her on the couch. At that moment Ronnie said that she had an important telephone call to make and the two of them could get acquainted.

The man, who seemed to be in his early fifties, told her,

'Ronnie said you would be fresh and innocent and a knockout.'

Inez didn't understand. 'I have two children. How innocent can I be?'

He ignored her question, instead moved closer, so that his leg touched her thigh. Inez shifted away but the man stuck close. 'Oh,' he told her, 'I can see the innocence in you; it's something more than in your body, it can be in your mind. I mean one can tell you're the kind of woman who gives to a man only when she really wants to.'

He spoke almost clinically. Inez didn't follow her first inclination, which was to be insulted. As a matter of fact, she felt complimented.

The older man let his words sink in, then took Inez's hands in his almost paternally, patting them, allowing one hand to touch her knee.

'You see,' he went on softly, 'Ronnie told me you might not understand.'

'I don't really understand,' Inez answered, at the same time wondering where Ronnie was.

'Well,' he continued, 'I'm an old friend of Ronnie's. She's been good to me. Been kind of lonesome for me with out my wife. She seems to be able to do the right thing at the right moment. Introducing you to me is one of them.*

'Thank you,' Inez told him, not quite knowing what else to say.

'Fimny,' the man went on, moving his body directly against her, letting his fingers touch her shoulder. 'I bought my first wife everything, everything she wanted. It wasn't enough.'

'It wasn't?' Inez asked.

'No, she left. I never knew that what I could do for her wasn't enough. She had only to ask.'

Inez sighed and the man let his fingers catch the firm outline of her breast. Inez shuddered but the man didn't remove his hand.

'Yes, I would try, as tired as I was, I would try.'

'How awful,' Inez murmured, forgetting that it was the

middle of the afternoon, forgetting that Ronnie had not returned.

The man became more affectionate, more sure of what he was doing. He let his fingers trail along her ungirdled body, feeling the pliable skin, the legs bunching together as if to close out any access. He was patient but firm, disregarding her protestations, pulling her around to him, feeling her brushing her breasts with his mouth. He kissed her wet and full, sucking her lips, making her amorous. Without real ising she was going. Inez allowed herself to halffollow, half lead the man across the room and through an open door which he closed quietly behind him.

In another moment she was on the bed and he was beside her, pulling down the back zipper of her dress, quieting her protests, which became weaker and weaker. He was beside her in bed, each feeling the other's coolness, the others warmth.

Inez wanted to scream for him to hurry. But she had the feeling he would not disappoint her. Indeed he didn t. She felt his mouth on her neck, his kisses on her bare breasts.

She closed her eyes.

There was a moment of elation she had never felt before.

She thought her breath changed; her puke was beating out of her skin, her body quivering and moving, as if a fare would start from the friction. The fire within....

Then it was quiet. She remained with her eyes closed. It seemed a moment later. When she opened them the man was gone Inez dressed quickly and went out of the room, ready to sneak out of the house. But Ronnie was in the living room sipping a brandy. In a comer she saw another woman sitting in the shadows.

'Oh, sweetie; Ronnie told her. 'wait inside. I want to talk to you.'

In a moment Ronnie joined her and held out a packet of bills. 'Here, thirty five dollars. I've taken my share off the top.'

'I don't understand.'

'Well, you told me you couldn't type, didn't know what kind of a job you were suited to. I knew the one you'd be suited for. I find out that if it happens the first time like this, sort of natural, it's easier the second time. You can come here as often as you like, stay as long as you like.'

Slowly it hit Inez what Ronnie was talking about.

'You want me to be a .' She couldn't get the word out

Ronnie answered, 'You needn't get holier than thou. After all, I know what happened. So we're not talking about what you would do, but what you can do to make money.'

'And you, too.'

'Of course, me too,' Ronnie answered, 'that's the way it is.'

On her way home Inez stopped to buy an expensive cut of steak for dinner that evening. It was the sort of cut they had never indulged in. She still had enough money left over to buy a blouse that she had long admired.

That night her husband enjoyed the steak but asked puzzledly how she could have afforded it out of the tight food budget. In the evening she lay in bed with him as he perfunctorily made love to her. The next afternoon Inez paid another visit to Ronnie. This time she stayed later.

What Inez didn't know was that her activities were not

unique; they are carried on in many suburbs throughout the country. She began to suspect that other women were getting new dresses and second cars by doing what she was. She bought clothes, explained a few hundred dollars as winnings at a church bingo game.

The My Life Is Hell At Home Game which began with her feelings of deprivation was now continuing though with immense feelings of guilt. But each pang was assuaged by the money she received, if not from the different character of the lovemaking.

Of course if she truly had allowed her husband to make love to her as she had these strangers he might very well have been a totally different person. True she reached climaxes of gratification, chills that resulted from being explored as her body had never been before, gradually accepting any activity as equal to the increasing fee she received, explaining the bruises on her body to her husband as accidental falls. And indeed they were. In turn she learned to turn. the trick, to face a man with only temporary indifference, and not to face him, to turn her head and body and make herself available, to twist her face and go south or north and travel the road to more money for herself.

It is probable that Inez will be found out, as other women have been, by probing police and district attorneys. She may even be indicted for criminal activities when, in fact, she was playing a game.

The My Life Is Hell At Home Game is based on many diverse factors, depending on the needs of the woman. In Feminine Superiority and Other Myths Arnold H. Kamiat says that women 'have pursued power and material wealth, they have been just as selfish and egotistic as men, and many have on occasion resorted to violence and to crime ...' The author goes on to add that 'Women are egotistic, selfaggrandising, tyrannous, domineering creatures, creatures to be feared....' Whether the writer's divorce had anything to do with his unusually hard judgments, he is reiterating the old saying that hell hath no fury like a woman scorned and adding abused, mistreated, left out of things, not catered to and other neglects.

While The My Life Is Hell At Home Game may be the parent of many adventures, the number one offspring would be The Let's Have An Affair Game.

This last is more a subgame than a primary one. It has been said that American woman, since frontier times onward to the beginning of the twentieth century, was notable for fighting for her man. Of late it would appear the American woman expends greater energy in fighting against him. She just doesn't fight against him for the pure joy of doing battle, although many feminists would have us believe that, but often uses some excuse to bolster her for doing battle. 'My husband doesn't understand me and besides he's a beast' is as good as any reason.

For some, divorce isn't the answer for reasons of religion. For others, despite all the real and imagined abuses, there is a form of security in marriage. If an extramarital affair is regarded as a game, however, by both partners, it might take on an aura of respectability. The rise of wifeswapping clubs, which offer opportunities for mutual sexual indulgence, may be one recourse. As one twentyoneyearold wife of a carpenter writes: 'This was something we had only heard about and were very happy finally to be invited to one (a wifeswapping session). You know my husband and I hadn't been getting along too well, I mean he couldn't satisfy me and I, to be honest, couldn't make him feel too good. Anyway we went; We didn't know any of the people who were going to be there and I felt funny about it. At first we just sat and talked to some of the couples. Then after a while things really started moving. It was a very small place with a lot of people so there were couples all over the place. Some were just talking while others were making love right in front of us. I was a little shocked at first but then got into the swing of things. I found that I was enjoying myself very much and just wanted to keep going and haven't stopped yet.'

This young thing, not the most beautiful girl in the world, and perhaps not the brightest, was playing The My Life Is Hell At Home Game. But she was wise enough to play it with her husband. She'd be damned if she'd be satisfied with a small messy apartment, an inadequate wardrobe and the frustration of having her husband, animallike, grab her, love her, and quickly cast her aside. She didn't have enough money for a divorce. Nor did that thought ever occur to her. As with so many of her education and upbringing, there was an almost sad willingness to live in perpetual hell. As long as hell could be mitigated by a bit of heaven.

Although the parties allowed her husband to gratify himself the young bride still thought she was putting something over on him. She had always thought that a man would be unfaithful no matter what. So, that he was indulging in every sexual excess with other women was not in itself shocking. She had given it her blessing. But that she too was given equal time to have sex outside marriage and to do it with his permission was, in her mind, a tremendous trick. If life was hell at home, she was finding her own heaven with his blessing and cooperation.

If there is any desire common to most of the women who play The My Life Js Hell At Home Game it is revenge. Sometimes it seems hardly conscious. Other times it takes on aspects of malice. Such was the case of Linda R. Linda's husband was a presser in a dry cleaners. They had been married for a few years, were still in their early twenties, and completely trapped by their inability to get ahead financially, their inability to express themselves either fully or adequately, socially and sexually. They had no children, lived in what was termed a lowincome apartment, and had, by most standards a drab, inconsequential life. They lived in the farout suburbs of New York City, each commuting to his job by a long and tortuous subway and bus ride.

Linda was a plain girl. She wore the latest short skirts and stark makeup with less success than they were designed to accomplish. She was aware of it. For this reason she was resigned to having married a man, any man, it seemed. She never thought of her husband as being particularly handsome. Certainly his habits around the house made him less than attractive. The sight of him walking around in undershirt and slacks, swilling beer out of the can while watching a ball game on television conjured up no romantic notions.

Linda's job was as receptionist for an industrial concern. She met a long flow of salesmen each day. So anxious were they to make sure they would get in to see the buyer they took to Haltering Linda. Once in a while she would receive a box of candy, or flowers, and once, tickets for a show. Her husband wasn't interested in going and wouldn't hear of her going alone or with a girl friend. She had to give them away. It was weeks before she forgave him for that.

However the constant flow of attention she received was mistaken for something personal rather than a game the salesmen played. It bolstered Linda's ego, made her able to face her husband and at the same time wish for something more. As the weeks went on the attention only served to dramatise how dull her home life really was.

Linda knew no escape. She lived in a sort of purgatory, waiting for either heaven or hell but pretty sure in which direction she was heading. Each new day she dreamed that something exciting would happen to get her out of the rut. She had neither the intellect nor the imagination to arrange a way out. Nevertheless, the growing passion to do something exciting got in the way of every thought she had.

Her opportunity came very simply. One day her husband brought a friend home for supper. He hadn't told her and didn't apologise for the unexpected company.

Timmy was a year older than Linda, a tall, goodlooking fellow who worked with her husband. He was single, lived alone and had only recently moved to New York.

'If we had room, I'd like to put you up here,' her husband told him after supper.

Tirnmy answered, 'Maybe Linda would object.'

'Oh,' her husband answered, 'Linda does what I tell her.'

He gave his wife a gentle slap across the bottom.

Linda washed the dishes and prolonged the task to stay out of the living room as long as possible. She could hear the two of them telling dirty jokes, and laughing uproarously. But mostly her husband did the telling and the laughing Timmy and her husband drank beer with Timmy nursing one to the other man's two. Linda only went through the living room to go to the bathroom. She walked fast. a bit selfconscious of the stranger who was visiting. She was still shy in spite of marriage and working.

As she walked past, Timmy said, 'Why don't you join us I mean, I hope I didn't spoil anything. If I did I'm sorry, 1 really didn't want to come without calling you. Anyway, it was a good meal.'

Linda stopped long enough to thank him for the unac customed flattery. As she was making up her face m the bathroom she realised that she had never made up for her husband. She knew she was doing it for Timmy and the thought made her feel wicked and tempting. She straightened her dress, adjusted her hose and went to join the men.

Her husband had fallen asleep, his shoes off, one leg across the chair. .

'He works hard,' Timmy said. Linda knew it was the beer. It did it to him every time.

They talked a while of ordinary things, where he came from, what he wanted to do.

This job is only a beginning. I'll get some experience and move on. But one thing, your husband has been a good friend, shown me the ropes. I mean I couldn't have kept the job without him. He's a real nice guy.'

'Sure he is; Linda nodded, looking at her sleeping

husband.

A few moments later Timmy said he had to leave, pausing in the doorway just long enough to kiss Linda lightly on the forehead. 'That's for a nice supper and not complaining. I hope to see you again.'

'I hope so, too.' She held out her hand and he shook it, letting his finger drag across her palm, making her feel the touch right down her spine.

Later that night, in bed. she told her husband, 'I like your friend. He's so polite.'

'Yeh,' he answered beerily, he's strange, damn polite. I'll have to tell him to cut that out. He might spoil you.'

Linda tried to be affectionate withher husband. But right after talking he turned on his side and started to snore.

'Damn,' she said, loud enough to wake him, she hoped. But he didn't hear her. She kicked him under the blanket but he only made a small grunt and continued snoring.

The next morning they argued from the minute they awoke. Linda complained about the apartment, her clothes, his job, how much money they had, the fact that she had to go to work. She complained about everything except the underlying reason, her unfulfilhnent as a woman.

'Well maybe I shouldn't invite Timmy again, to see and hear you bitching like this.'

'Oh no,' she stopped short, 'why not bring him? It will be nice to have a man around the house.'

Her husband didn't get insulted. He almost never took anything she said personally. 'Yeh, maybe he could teach you a few things.'

Linda knew her husband was joking. She wasn't,

however, when she answered, 'I'd love to learn.'

There was a Greek who wrote: 'Formerly a woman was silent and shy during the wedding night but now a woman gives herself to the first handsome coachman she sees . . . Virtue has disappeared; ungodliness, treachery and sensua lism are rife everywhere.' That wasn't said just yesterday. Ptirim Sorokin in his book The American Sex Revolution quotes an ancient Macedonian who made that complaint 2,000 years ago. Sorokin, incidentally, also commented that 'Since a notable proportion of our women and men are infected by the sex obsession, and since they marry hastily and overvalue the sex love in their married life, many of them are frequently tempted to indulge in extramarital liaisons.'

In other words when life at home is hell, play the game. Linda was ready. She didn't know it, but she had already started to play.

Her real opportunity came when her husband was out bowling and Timmy happened by.

'I thought this was the night I was to come for supper. I guess it's tomorrow.' ,

'That's all right,' she told him, 'come in and wait. He U be back from bowling in a couple of hours.'

The next two hours were all she had, she reasoned. She had two hours in which to become a woman. She offered Timmy a beer, made him some sandwiches and asked him if he liked music. She put a record on, turned down some of the lights and, excusing herself, went into the bedroom, changed her dress, put some perfume where she thought it would be the most effective, brought out a new record and sat beside him to show him the album cover.

She knew that her breasts were rising and falling, that the perfume must have been noticed, that she felt warm and that that warmth had crossed from her to Timmy. He took the album and his hand touched hers. She leaned over to point something out and her breast brushed his arm. Timmy started to move away but the end of the couch stopped him.

Linda's bravura was something new, something uncontrollable. Without thinking why, she had taken Timmy's hand and placed it on her lap. His fingers then knew what to do, slowly crushing her dress to her body, convulsing her insides, her breath competing with the aroma of the perfume for attention, her body twisting and turning, her breasts desiretaut, the small laughter tussling brought to them not interfering with his quest for her entire body. In a moment she had slipped free of her clothing, showing her body, the small but full breasts, the cool white backside, crying for him to go on, not stop.

Timmy didn't excuse what he was doing with a friend's wife. He reacted as the sweetness assailed his nostrils, as the powdered body, in accord, blended with his. There was a gentleness and a harshness all at once. He was gentle as he caressed her face and firm as he stroked her legs.

They lay together on the couch, Linda not hearing her own breath, not smelling her own perfume as the aroma of musk masked it and the mansweat covered it. She was tired and fulfilled and in that moment only thought how much she hated her husband. The idea made her smile and press her lips together.

Timmy asked, 'Again?'

When she didn't answer he graduated and got his diploma, as for the second time Linda agitated her body and twisted her form and spirit. Timmy was using the tools of his trade as they should be, not unattended in his tool box as her husband's were. This construction took some moments longer, but the building was allimportant, the waiting for what she now knew she had a right to expect and she oohed and aahed aloud it being her only way of saying thank you.

Then Timmy was dressed and telling her, 'I'm not sorry I missed him.'

And Linda found herself answering, 'He goes bowling twice a week,' and mentioned the nights.

Timmy laughed. 'I could miss him then, too.'

'Yes, you could.' She kissed him and held on to him for a moment.

There were more moments to come for Linda. She could play out the game now, sweeter still with a friend of her husband's. In time Timmy would move. He had told her so. Linda would have to find another friend. This time she might not be so patient and wait for him to come to the house.

This is no sophisticated wandering. Therefore the results might be more dramatic than a divorce. Her husband might react physically, violently, so being the order of his class and experience.

But Linda takes a chance with The My Life Is Hell At Home Game played in all its basic animal simplicity. If she gets hit she won't be surprised, and probably not deterred from continuing.

Linda was sick of her life, but there is another woman whose sickness is not so easily defined. This is better explained and played in The Hypochondriac Game.

Chapter Eight

THE HYPOCHONDRIAC GAME

The whining, complaining, bellyaching, pilltaking wife has long been caricatured in books, films and the theatre. There is a method to her illness, a pleasure principle involved in her cries of pain. Don't dismiss the feigned ailments as looking for sympathy. That's too pat an answer. Certainly psychiatric and other medical treatment would provide profound and professional answers. But it is not stretching hypothesis too far to suggest that a sick woman in bed always keeps a husband away and at home at the same time. It certainly will keep him out of the conjugal bed, while making him an attentive slave to her wishes.

Although it frequently is, as George Bernard Shaw said in Man and Superman'... a woman's business to get married as soon as possible and a man's to keep unmarried as long as he can' some wives just cannot be satisfied with winning.

Probably the most insidious of all the games played by women is The Hypochondriac Game. Here she relies on a man's sympathy, public condemnation for leaving or being unfaithful to a "sick' wife, and even the court's reluctance to allow him to get a divorce.

What a woman might not reckon with, of course, is that her own natural desire, subdued as it is, might cause her to blow the game. In deliberately keeping'her husband away and at the same time suggesting how much she really needs him, she can play havoc with the urges within. As Theodor Reik said in Of Love and Lust, 'The sex urge hunts for lustful pleasure; love is in search of joy and happiness.' Or as one man puts it whimsically, 'I didn't know what real happiness was until I got married then it was too late.'

Individuals who don't give much thought to the reasons why the wife pretends to be ill might dismiss her with the comment, 'She seems to enjoy ill health.' Maybe so. Meanwhile she's hooked the poor guy, has him tied down until one or the other dies.

Grace F. was such a wife. Married at nineteen, a mother at twenty, and a mother again at twentyone. Grace spent nearly all the following twenty years in bed. Her husband had a small variety store, made a comfortable living, worked long hours, was able to send both his kids to college, and pay for a fulltime practical nurse to take care of his ailing wife.

They lived in Seattle, Washington. On occasion Mr F. would stand on the hill overlooking Puget Sound and wonder if there wasn't some freighter he could hop to escape from the trap in which his wife had bound him. He no longer doubted that she was truly ill. He rationalised that she must be to have kept it up so long. He didn't know that Grace had forced herself into a union with him and had borne two children with the most controlled horror and fear. When the second child was bom she told herself she had enough, enough children, enough sex, enough pawing by this man, who although her legal husband, she considered a stranger.

In the loneliness of her room. Grace would get out of bed and look in the mirror. She imagined she saw a homely, driedup woman, one who was unappealing and plain looking; in fact, rather repulsive.

This was far from the truth, but her belief encouraged her to keep her husband away without guilt. She imagined she was doing him a favor by not permitting him to feel he had to sleep with her.

Mr F. worked more than he had to, remained scrupulously faithful and even indulgent to his wife. He kept his own pains and ailments to himself. So it was that one month before their twentythird wedding anniversary he died suddenly of a heart attack.

Friends and relatives assumed the shock would be too much for Grace. But safe in the knowledge now that he could no longer physically attack her, she got out of bed and attended the funeral. Everyone thought she showed so much courage.

For the next year Grace went out, slowly adapting herself to the outside world. She met a widower about her own age who lived with his young niece. They went out on simple, innocent dates, with no stronger contact than handholding at the movies. The day he proposed Grace accepted without thinking.

The wedding night was a horror. It was then that Grace realised what she had done to herself, that it was starting all over again. Nick was a good catch, more so for a widow her age, everyone told her. Yet, comparing herself to his eighteenyearold niece Joy, Grace felt old and haggard. Joy was fresh, freeswinging, looked fine in hiphugging pants and tight sweaters. Grace was only too aware that Nick regarded his niece with fondness and he hugged her with what seemed undue warmth. On the wedding night as Nick came to join her in bed she shut her eyes tight, made a grimace with her mouth and offered her new husband no help at all. He mistook her passiveness for something natural from a widow who had 'loved' her first husband very much. Grace wanted him so much it hurt. Still she was frightened and revolted by the act. She told Nick she had a headache; not to hurry because she would be his wife for a long time.

As patient as he was, he was not to be denied, and he told her, 'I understand. But try.'

She lay there, feeling his warmth close in over her, allowing her breasts to be mauled, her back to be scratched, her flanks to be pulled closer to him. How can he want me? she thought to herself. I'm so old and so ugly.

As if to answer her unspoken question, she heard him say, 'You are beautiful, with a figure I never imagined.'

It was no use, she realises, he was going to go ahead as if he didn't care about her. She tried to talk but was stopped by his mouth swarming over hers. She felt him aim and expected the trigger to be squeezed, now that it was cocked. Her eyes, which had been closed, opened wide, staring at him through the dim light. What she said was not pre determined, although the result was just what she had hoped. She looked at him as he strained and tried to prolong that which he wanted to happen, but slowly and delieiously. 'You look,' she said almost whimsically, 'so strange and funny.'

What happened was that he stopped short, feeling altogether stupid and angry at the same time.

Grace told him, 'I'll be better in the morning, dear.'

Nick had heard about her long illness but had not doubted that it was over. But now he realised he had been trapped. The story he had heard about her first husband's slavelike devotion would be his story, too. He just didn't know what to do about it.

For weeks. Grace stayed in bed, her food brought up to her room by Joy. The young girl was genuinely attentive but her presence only served to remind Grace of what she thought was her own lack of appeal. It strengthened her illness, made her cureday more distant.

Then Grace took to dreaming that she was Joy, that she was the young and uninhibited girl who swung her hips with abandon, whom she had seen parading in front of the bath room mirror when she thought no one else was looking. She had seen her kiss her uncle. Grace's husband, as a lover and not a niece.

In her dreams Grace was in Joy's body cavorting with Nick chasing him nude around the bedroom, catching him, playing with his penis, fondling every part of him, screeching with delight as he caught her, sipped on her breasts, and petted her, carried her, whimpering, to the marriage bed. She thanked him so many times it sounded like a benediction.

The Hypochondriac Game is often the manifestation of deeper and more serious problems. Grace had begun to think of herself as young and seductive as Joy. It was more than a dream. She was Joy in body and spirit. Yet she knew she was Grace and her desire to be Joy was coupled with her desire for Nick to want her.

It happened one night, many months after her 'illness' had overtaken her, that Nick was sitting on the edge of the bed. Joy had gone out for the evening. He had put his arm around her, as he had often done, expecting nothing more than an acknowledging pat that he was there. Instead, Grace reached around and drew him to her, kissing him on the mouth, watering his lips, planting her tongue inside him. At first surprised. Nick let her, then without question responded, falling down beside his wife who seemed now not at all like the woman he had married.

Her body was shapely, solid, not at all flabby but firm; strong in spite of the inactivity; full and mature unlike any simple child's. Her face had been powdered and there was makeup on her eyes, something he now noticed for the first time. The gentle aroma of perfume reached his nostrils. He knew the body and the shape of Grace, but the affection, the tickling of his ribs, the gentle grasp of his body. the slow caress of his back, was another woman's a younger woman who was joining him. Yet he saw Grace. She made no slight ing remarks. She said nothing that would discourage him.

Her every act was designed to increase his expectation,

to bring nearer his goal, to keep it just remote enough to be felt, twist and turn him in the right direction, catching the ebb and flow of his body movements with a dexterity that was expert in its control, sympathetic in its understanding, and mutually desirous.

'Oh my dear Nick, my dear Nick. I am so glad that you are everywhere, that I can surround you, encase you, hold you within, trapped and for me.'

He had never heard Grace talk like this. The words sounded much like those in the books she had been reading about romanceatthetumofthecentury. Nevertheless he was grateful. He didn't question her. He covered her breasts with kisses, the gently rounded belly, the soft moons of her buttocks, the stretching aching groin. . . . And then he joined her with all the passion he could muster, barely able to keep up with her. They enjoyed a mutual orgasm that made the past loveless months well worth the waiting.

Once it was over the woman lay back. Now she was Grace, tired and afraid. When Nick tried to caress her again she told him she ached. Puzzled, he got up from the bed.

For weeks after Grace lay ill (or so she told him), but Nick was patient. Then one night she was Joy again and her illness disappeared and was replaced by joyous lovemaking, both oral and otherwise.

Grace played the game with consummate skill. She was able to be sick when it pleased her and loving when that held her interest. In her mind it was not Grace who indulged herself sexually, it was Joy, another Joy who looked like and seemed like her husband's niece.

The Hypochondriac Game had gotten out of hand. It

was played with passion and zeal to cover up her fear and reward her at the same time. Nick was never aware that he was let out and pulled back as some fish caught on a long line, allowed to swim away for only a short distance, brought back as the fisherman deemed fit.

Nick's sexual ebb and flow was both satisfying and discomforting. He cursed when he was rebuffed and enjoyed pleasures no man could imagine at other times. So much so that he told his wife one night, 'Sometimes I think I married a girl who lied about her age. Deliberately told me she was older. You must be fooling me.'

He wondered why, after what he thought was a compliment, Grace froze up, twisted her knees together, locked him out and kept him away for weeks.

Their marriage is succeeding in spite of Grace's intermittant illnesses, or perhaps because of them. Grace plays The Hypochondriac Game with the strength of a martyr and stops only when the greater strength of a woman's sex needs overtakes her.

The Hypochondriac Game played in its most simplistic form is the wife who says Tm too tired' or the girl friend who hesitates with Td let you in but I've got this terrible headache,' or the little bitch who had you spend more than you intended, drank more than you thought possible, and leaves you sexually frustrated at the door.

Sometimes the girl reasons that she will take the slob for a ride and not get hung up. At other times, the game may be played out of sheer perversity or temporary fear.

A girl, or a grown woman for that matter, can be so obsessed with fear of what a man will do that she will resort to any number of pretexts though never to avoid him completely to keep him. As Simone de Beauvoir commented in The Second Sex, The thought of appearing nude before a man overwhelms her with excitement but she feels she will be helpless under bis gaze ... but the most obvious and the most detestable symbol of physical possession is penetration by the sex organ of the male.'

It is the ambivalence and contradiction in goals that makes the conflict so stark, as De Beauvoir further adds,'. . . she cannot become grown up without accepting her femininity; and she knows already her sex condemns her to a mutilated and fixed existence....'

Ariene was a tease in high school, a tease in college, and a tease on the job. She was a rarity; a virgin' despite handsome young men bent on debauchery, excesses of alcohol and the influence of raging, sensuous music.

Ariene was a distinctive young woman who combined an excess of voluptuous good looks with a brimming, yet subdued intellect. She was more than a healthy mmd in a healthy body; she was a wild, free body, controlled by an active, if confused intellect.

For a while she had thought that her refusal to go beyond the petting stage was due to an imbalance in her hormones, more male than female, in spite of her looks; or due to some traumatic shock from early childhood. She had tried psychiatric help. but fought the doctor and soon gave it up.'

On the surface she seemed to be getting the most out of life. But she was not only frustrating the men who took her , out, but causing deep anguish in herself as she fought impulses she reasoned must be natural, all the while she pushed them aside.

Ariene had come to New York City from San Francisco. Usually the first question she was asked was why anyone would want to leave the scene of Haight Ashbury, the Hill. the waterfront, the excitement that was generated in the Bay area for New York City. Part of Ariene's reason for leaving was to escape, to take flight from the omnipresent sexual freedom that surrounded her. When she had gone out on a date she ended up in someone's apartment. She was tired of making up reasons why she wouldn't smoke pot or join anyone on a fast trip; instead of freaking out she was freaked. Ariene had had the chasing and the pawing and the clawing. Whenever a man kissed her she was overwhelmed with nausea that, real or imagined, brought on a headache or stomach cramps. No matter what the pain, she was able to wrench herself free and be taken home. No seductionbent swain was going to enjoy forcing himself on a girl, even one as sensuouslooking as Ariene, while she had the dry heaves and he expected to be vomited out of the place.

Arlene's circle of acquaintances was inbred. So much so that when she was a repeat date the fellow was playing the odds that he would penetrate the impenetrable, break a path through the maze that was the forest of her confusion. Arlene had no compunctions about wearing short skirts, so that when she bent over the lace trim of her panties, always dark, accented the white of her thigh, or the transparent panty hose showed the place where the journey would end. She wore blouses that clung over unbrassiered breasts, that tormented the viewer and might allow him to realise the shape and the feel of their contours but could never be removed from the shelf. Once Arlene teased one man who would have raped her had she not swung a handy stick.

Arlene didn't wait to get home before feeling her headache pains: She waited until dessert, until the check had been paid, or until he had called a cab. But her illnesses finally discouraged her dates. It was then that she cut out and came to New York.

She lived alone, had no desire to share an apartment. She thought she might get professional help to cure the gnawing at her innards but decided against it. Arlene had a responsible position with an advertising agency and had no problem in getting dates. But she did have a problem in keeping them coming back.

The Hypochondriac Game is easily recognised for what it is, a ploy, a delaying action. In Arlene's case the delay was interminable. She agreed with Dr L. Clendenning who had written in The Human Body that man's sole purpose in life was to roam over the earth making as many females pregnant as possible. Arlene used this as an excuse which brought on stomach pains, chills, headaches, imagined symptoms of her fear. But she was bright enough to know it must end if she was ever to feel fulfilled as a woman.

There was no doubt that Arlene was playing The Hypochondriac Game against her most earnest wishes. She just couldn't work up courage to let nature take its course. At the last moment she felt ill, or at least said that she did. Her life might have continued along this strange, frustrating course if she hadn't met Johnny.

Johnny D. was in his late thirties and had traveled around the world as a reporter and war correspondent. He had trafficked with the prostitutes of Indonesia, the women in the windows of Hamburg, Germany, had unveiled an Arab's woman and barely escaped with his life. Johnny had witnessed and taken part in Turkish orgies, bathed with the Japanese, slept with a Greek rebel's woman, and openly espoused Scandinavian sexual freedom. There was nothing he needed less than a promiscuous woman, there was nothing he wanted more than a bright, intelligent woman with whom he could feel intellectually as well as physically compatible.

He met Arlene at a cocktail party right after she had com plained of standard headache number one. Her date was a rising young advertising agency executive who was as disgusted with her illness as he had been infatuated with her body. Johnny had overheard her complain and offered to take her home.

Johnny was in no mood for sex, though he would not have slammed shut an open door. He was physically tired. had a headache himself from listening to the partygoer's small talk.

In the cab home he sat to one side, Arlene to the other.

He made no attempt to come closer. After introducing him self, he had said, 'I have a headache too. From listening to those nitwits talk about things they don't know anything about. They think making a new bar of soap is great. Maybe it is for them. But they give me a pain right here. How's your head?'

Arlene smiled. 'Surprisingly, it's feeling better.

'Maybe you'd like to stop for a cup of coffee?'

She agreed and he told the cab to pull up. They walked

to an allnight cafeteria, had. coffee and pie. They talked about the places he had been. a little bit about what she did. She was fascinated by the countries he had visited. He was fascinated by the fact that she was a good listener. After about an hour he took her home, asked for her phone number and said he might call again. Arlene said she hoped he would. That night she slept without pain, without any fear or feeling of selfrecrimination.

Johnny called back in about two weeks. They met for dinner. He had returned from an assignment. They spent a couple of hours together. He was physically exhausted, having flown in from a combat area that same day. He apologised for taking her home early but said that he simply couldn't stay awake any more. If he hadn't wanted to see her so much he would have gone straight home to bed. Alone. ,

Arlene didn't hear from Johnny for another three weeks. Again the pattern repeated itself. She wondered if he really was all that tired, or was there something wrong with him? It never occurred to her that his actions mirrored her own on previous dates. What she did feel, however, was a grow ing doubt as to her femininity. She'd leave Johnny, undress, stare in the mirror at her shapely figure and think she was too fat, look at her face with its wide, appealing eyes and moist mouth and find it plain. She looked at her firm, pliant legs and thought them too big. She went to bed with a recur rance of her earlier headaches. Only this time the pain was more intense, and the reason had changed. Where before she had feigned illness to keep a man away. The Hypochondriac Game had reversed itself and the pain in her gut, the ache m her head were strengthened because one man kept away.

It was almost a month before she heard from Johnny again. He had been covering a revolution, going through hell without sleep for days on end, had lost weight, and returned to the States physically exhausted. He called Arlene because he enjoyed her company. She made no demands on him and he appreciated that he could be with a woman without having to, or being expected to, climb into bed with her.

When Arlene met him this time she dressed extra carefully, listened to him politely. When there was a pause, she asked: *You do like me. Johnny?'

He nodded.

'Then why do you treat me like a sister?'

°I don't know what you mean.'

'I'm reasonably attractive. You haven't made a pass. Is it a game? Are you just stringing me along, then pow, I'm supposed to come crawling to you?'

He was genuinely surprised. 'No, dammit, no. You know the hell I've been going through. I've been selfish, only thinking of myself. Sure, I think of you as a woman, a beautiful woman, but maybe I'm thinking of how exhausted I am. I'll show you/ he got up. 'Let's go home.'

In the cab Johnny put his arm around her and kissed her. She felt him stiffen and his mouth grow warm.

When they got out of the cab she hurried ahead of him to open the apartment door, the demands of the waiting making her hurry. Her body ached and itched with a different kind of intensity. Johnny had hardly closed the door behind him when he caught her in his arms, swung her about with all the passion he had suppressed. He held her, bit her lips until she let out a small shriek. He tossed her on the bed, forgetting his own tiredness, his own physical pain. Arlene tried to get away but he refused to let her, in the process ripping off her brandnew dress. She struggled free and ran across the room.

'You bitch,' he barked. 'You asked me. Here I am.

He caught her in a corner, pulling off her bra, staring at the most beautiful body he had seen in a long time.

'You're clean and you smell like a woman, not like those filthy bitches I've been with.'

She cowered in the corner as he reached for her. In trying to push him away she grabbed at his pants. He mistook her fear for desire and laughed. 'If I had known this was the kind of game you wanted to play I wouldn't have wasted so much time.'

Then as suddenly as he had been fierce, a gentleness overcame him. He picked Arlene up and carried her into the bedroom, placed her gently down on the bed, and began to caress and kiss every part of her body while she writhed and kicked.

Johnny stepped back a moment, staring at her. Arlene both wanted and didn't want the moment to come. She put her hand across her eyes. In that moment the pains came back to her head, the ache in her groin became the ache in her temples, the throbbing m her gut became a throbbing in her head.

'Oh Johnny,' she whimpered, 'I have such a headache. I ...' She started to cry and sounded as if she were going to retch.

The guttural sounds sobered Johnny. He realised how

beat he was. It had not been long since he had had a woman, so he said, 'Okay, I understand. But I'm sure you've been making up what you've been missing from me. You'd be a damn fool if you wasted what you have.'

She heard the words and could only moan, 'Oh Johnny.'

He mistook the cry for meaning she wished she could be with him. He patted her and said next time.

But Arlene knew there would be no next time. Johnny left and the night was over.

The next day she made an appointment with a psychiatrist. She was tired of playing. If she couldn't change the game, she wanted to know how to change the rules. The chances are she'll be able to do both.

One shouldn't think that The Hypochondriac Game need be so complex. It can be played as the mood strikes. When the girl says she has a headache, it is no matter whether it is real or imaginary. For many reasons or for no reason at all it may be used as an excuse. Sometimes it is to put a man in his place. Only the weak and the timid will not find a cure for the headache.

The Hypochondriac Game may seem like negative entrapment, and it probably is. There is a more direct game that is played The Sensual Game.

Chapter Nine

THE SENSUAL GAME

It is easy for some guy to think that just because he's been able to seduce a girl on the very first night he's got the upper hand. Not necessarily so. Especially not if shes playing The Sensual Game. One might think that every game is sensual. Maybe so. But the rules of The Sensual Game put to use the very moods and desires that impel a woman to take up with a man. It is more fhan giving her body it is using her body. To the woman who plays this game the result is more important than any transient pleasure. To be sure, she won't knock what happens along the way. In this instance it just happens to be a very good bonus.

There are dangers to The Sensual Game. You can t lead every man on and on. Some get out of hand. As Albert Deutsch writes in Sex Habits of the American Male, 'Exten sive petting short of orgasm seriously disturbs some individuals, but perhaps a third are able to calm down after it.... Deutsch makes another comment relating to The Sensual Game 'If the male does not want marriage, he is apt to balance the costs of this courtship, and the uncertainties of its outcome, against the possibilities of "easier" girls.'

Let us suppose that some designing female, to use an ancient but accurate term, wants to get a man to commit a crime, get her some clothes, do her a favor or even do a favor for a boy friend: She can use her body if that is the only weapon at hand.

History is replete with women who have played The Sensual Game, from Cleopatra who flirted with Caesar and Marc Antony to the latest Hollywood starlet. Sheba tempted Solomon, Delilah destroyed Samson and a little girl from a small town in Vermont tempted a television producer right out of his job .

Zena was the first name she used. It wasn't her real name but it sounded important and that was all that mattered to this young thing who came down from the cold country to warm up the big city.

Zena had graduated from high school, cadged a few hundred dollars from her father and taken the tram to Manhattan. She checked in at a women's hotel and planned her Steen Zena had the cool and emulative cunning of a woman twice her age. She checked her assets. Her face to one. Heartshaped, set off by straight hair and wide brown

yes. Her body for another. Full where it should be and round in back. Her legs, trim and firm. She was fivethree not too short and not too tall. she thought. What she planned to do was take each of these assets and combine them mto a major striking force. Zena was determined to go broke

She gave herself one month to succeed The odds would seem to be against her. She was a total stranger with no particular aptitude for employment, except perhaps he applause she had received in school plays. Yes, she reasoned, that was another asset.

Zena used her first day to look through the show business trade papers. She saw ads where figure models were wanted no experience necessary. It didn't take her long to find out this was a euphemism for nude modeling. She posed for a day, decided that it was a dead end, asked for her money brushed past the weaving fingers of the manager and walked out.She next modeled lingerie for a manufacturer who advertised in a number of the men's magazines. The merchandise was virtually transparent, what there was of it.

The husband and wife owners treated her as something less than human as she paraded before the buyers. She would have quit because this too appeared to be another dead end. However, the husband was a former actor who kept up with old friends still active in show business. That's how Zena met Marty, Actually Marty saw her first. She was modeling a blacklace bra that covered half her breasts with fabric and that half only wishfully. Zena sensed the merchandise was having an effect on Marty.

The producer asked her to have a drink in spite of his friend's warnings not to mix pleasure with business. But Marty told Zena to answer for herself and she said yes, of course.

They went to a nearby bar, had a couple of drinks and he asked her to go home with him. There was no beating around the bush, no small talk.

'You think what I have is worth something?' Zena asked.

'Sister, I don't pay for anything, not at this stage of my life,' he told her.

'Oh, honey, I don't want money from you, I want a break. K what I have is worth something, it's worth at least giving me a break.'

Marty was in his early forties. It was late and he was in no mood for games but he said, 'Okay, maybe. But what can you do?'

'Take me home,' she told him. 'I'll show you.'

His apartment was not far from where they were having their drinks. As soon as they were inside she stood before him, drew her foot back and forth, as if over an imaginary line. She laughed and dared him to come after her. Marty made a pass and she laughed again, dodging him. In running she tripped and he fell over her on to the floor. Still laughing she stilled his mouth with her fingers, then kissed his lower lip, pulling away as he went to put his arms around her. She allowed herself to be caught, covered his eyes with her hands and pushed her tongue into his mouth, moving it back and forth, then slowly withdrawing it until her mouth clung to his lips and she motioned for him to get up as she swayed, her body undulating, twisting back and forth, her mouth never leaving his, her lips closing on his. She arched out of reach and when he was about to grab her she backed away, laughed and heard him swear.

Zena lay down on the floor. Marty stared after her, not knowing what she would do next. She kicked off a shoe so that it sailed past his head. He continued to stare as she pushed off the other shoe, reached up her thighs to start to roll down her hose then motioned for Marty to take it off. She raised each leg so that her skirt fell back up to her waist as Marty gently rolled both stockings off and let them fall limply on to the carpet. The producer got down on the floor beside her, tried to put an arm around her but she rolled away, loosening her side zipper as she did, exposing white flesh, twisting the dress so that he would see her navel. When Marty reached over again she bit him on the side of the neck, quickly got to her feet and ran into the bathroom. She emerged in a moment without her dress. Slip and undies only. She got down on her knees and motioned for Marty to do the same. She made him kiss her nose. Marty reached around and unhooked her bra, dazzled by the sight of her nude breasts. It was all he could do to keep from raping her. But Zena got up and planted her feet astride and told him, 'What can you do for me?'

'I can get you an audition.'

'That's not enough,' she laughed, turned and bent over to pick up an imaginary piece of lint, showing him her backside, and peering between her legs she said, 'You have to get me a part.'

'Okay,' he reached for her, but she twisted away,

'Now,' she told him.

'Dammit, it's late.'

Zena pouted, 'Then I'm going home.' She began to pick up her clothes.

'Okay, I could make a call in the morning.'

She pointed to the phone, 'Why not now?'

Marty shrugged, reached for the phone and brought it

down to where he was sitting crosslegged on the floor. He apologised to the person at the other end for disturbing him. But he was able to guarantee that Zena would be given a bit part in a current production.

When he was through with the call Zena stretched out on the bed.

Zena's part ended up on the cutting room floor. Of course, she didn't receive any cheek. Then she discovered Marty was married.

'Oh, I never would have slept with you if I'd known that. I mean, it's all right for us to play a game together but I wasn't cheating on anyone the way you are.'

'What are you. a character out of a play?*

Zena was indignant, 'You cheated and I'm going to tell your wife and everybody else, too. You led me on.'

I led you on?'

'Yes, you did. You big creep.'

When Marty heard that Zena was making noises and accusations around the studio he took an assignment on the coast. He reached his wife before Zena did and sent her on a trip to the Bahamas.

Shortly thereafter Zena met another man, a director this time, who got her on a television panel show, as a guest on a network show, into a few motion picture parts. When he could do no more for her she dropped him.

One director led to the next. She was halfway through her twenties before the sheer pace of playing The Sensual Game began to take its toll. In this game the replacements come along faster than a hip can wiggle. Zena had had a short happy life. She was smart enough to realise it had run its course, so she married the next director she met.

Any mention of The Sensual Game without involving the most controversial of psychiatrists, Sigmund Freud, would be less than complete. Although much of Freud's emphasis on the general and specific domination of sex has been reinterpreted and reevaluated, without doubt he left his mark on all studies of human behaviour.

Freud was concerned not only with sex, but with sexuality as an overriding influence on all of men's activities. There is a type of woman who would play The Sensual Game with full knowledge of what she was doing, with the tacit endorsement of professionals. As Philip Rieff commented in Freud: The Mind of the Moralist, in the last of Three Essays Freud emphasised the fact 'that sexual excite ment, because it is a form of tension, must be counted as an unpleasurable feeling.' Rieff adds that'. . . only the act of discharge is acknowledged as genuine pleasure; the mutual caresses, however pleasant, which precede orgasm are purely anticipatory, the "forepleasure" which must be overcome.' Freud, of course advocated a doingaway of sexual repressions that associated the sex act with reproduction; at the same time, he believed this would relieve an individual from any 'moral horror now associated with perversion'.

Any individual who participates on a relatively exag gerated sex life may be considered an erotomaniac. The name given to men is satyriasist, to women nymphomaniac. It may very well be that a woman may have a difficult time in finding a man to satisfy her, so that to pin her with a label may be distinctly unfair. For as Sten and Inge Hegeler wrote in An ABZ of Love, 'We get so easily shocked by those who have more fun than we do ... and we have a tendency to regard what happens to be lovely, as unhealthy and sinful.'

Standards of society may so incessantly inhibit ones desire that playing a game is the only recourse. Queenie S. was forced into that situation. She left her native Australia at seventeen and emigrated to Canada. Because she came from Queensland her nickname was naturally assumed. Queenie was tall and languorous with straight hair that hung shawllike over her full body. She had a natural sway to her walk, a long thin waist, and the fullest of bosoms that seemed to defy natural laws in keeping her upright.

She worked for a while in Montreal as an assistant to a small printshop operator. When the man's wife found the two of them locked together amidst the pied type Queenie was forced to leave town. She worked at a number of odd jobs in small towns along the way to the States. In each instance her employment terminated with her insatiable desire for a man and her inability to keep from tempting him without regard for being found out. She compulsively twitted or taunted men and laughed when they were caught.

She soon tired of the intermittent pleasure, saved enough money for bus fare to New York City, and got a job handing out circulars to pedestrians in midtown Manhattan. It was winter and Queenie was wearing a fake mink coat. Under it she had on a panty and bra and nothing else. Whenever a man passed by she would fling open her coat, enabling him to get a good, quick glance at her exposed body, hand him a circular and show a smile. In no time she attracted a large crowd and with it the police. She was given a warning and fired by her employer. But it was not all bad. The producer of a local girlie show hired her to be a show girl, which involved nothing more than standing still during the show with relatively nothing on.

Queenie's playing The Sensual Game was done without specific desire for profit. Unlike Zena, Queenie had no long range plan, or shortrange aim for that matter, either. She was just interested in pursuing sex for its own sake. She became a 'character' with the show. Whenever the public relations man wanted a good press he would send Queenie out with a local gossip columnist, male, of course. Queenie was always good for a picture in the paper and a good notice for the show.

Her own attitude was so unaffected that every man who took her out believed that her behaviour was not an act. There is no telling how far Queenie might have gotten if she had had a goal and played The Sensual Game for some end.

The editor of a popular men's magazine was doing a feature on show girls. Queenie was brought to his attention. She told him of the jobs she had held, speaking in a littlegirl's voice. The editor figured that she might be star material. Perhaps Queenie could be promoted. What he didn't reckon with was Queenie's absolute lack of ambition. She was content with the meals he bought, the drinks she consumed. What disturbed her was that this editor seemed always concerned with business. She told him so.

'Karl,' she asked in her small voice, 'do you really think I can be a star?'

'Sure,' he answered, 'of course. You won't have to be standing in a line wearing pasties all the time. I've even been thinking that your voice would sound great on a record.'

'But then they couldn't see me,' she said innocently.

'Well, we could put you on the cover.'

'That would be nice. Karl,' she asked petulantly, 'don't you want to go to bed with me? I mean, I think maybe you're kind of strange.'

Karl laughed nervously. 'H you think I'm queer, I'm not.'

'Then how come you never made a pass at me?'

'I guess I figured it should be all business.'

She sounded indignant. 'That's pretty stupid. If this is all business is, I don't think I care to have anything to do with it.'

'Yeah, well,' he started to answer.

'You come with me to my hotel room and we can discuss business. I didn't know that was all that was holding you back.'

They left for her room. Queenie efficiently straightened out her bed, turned the lights down and began to play with the buttons on Kad's shirt, opening his clothing, telling him to be quiet and she would take care of everything.

She performed fellatio on him twice then, when he was reduced to a quivering mass of happy nerve endings, she, asked him for cunnilingus.

He was unwilling but in payment for her tender loving care and the promise that she would again do it to him he bent and, placing himself between her legs, he began to pay homage to her.

Queenie lay very still, immensely enjoying the act. She lay so still, in fact, he thought he was not pleasing her but she told him to continue while she fantasised. She was becoming more and more impassioned and finally when the right time came she jumped and howled like a banshee and poured forth her love into his mouth.

The next day Karl invested in renting a studio, hiring some writers to write a routine for Queenie and tried to convince himself he had found something in the strange girl. She eventually learned her lines, recorded a routine in that funny, childlike voice. When it was over she told Karl that it had been a lot of fun but that she was leaving New York for San Francisco or Chicago with a traveling burlesque company.

He argued with her that he had invested a great deal of time and money in preparing an act for her. Besides he had a contract that meant she had to stay.

Tm not your slave,' she told him. 'I can leave if I want

He waved the paper she had signed. It meant absolutely nothing to her. He reminded her of what they had done together.

Oh that.' she said, 'you were terrible. I could have had a really good time if you knew something. You know what I think you're pretty stupid.' She turned on her heels and started to leave his office.

Karl grabbed her and started to bring her back. He hesitated, stopped, returned to his desk. convinced that he had been had. He had had high hopes for profiting from Queenie as a personality.

Queenie, on the other hand, was playing The Sensual Game for its own sake. It didn't make a damn bit of differ. ence to her what happened, as long as there was a sexual outlet. Call her a nymphomaniac, but by whose standards Was she engaging in outlandish sex because she wanted to flaunt society's morals? Apparently not. She was one o those free people who have a need and a use for their Queenie, in her own way, was more honest than the housewife who takes up with her husband's best friend or the woman who deliberately sets out to cheat on a man. But because Queenie was simplistically honest didn't make her any the less dangerous. Queenie goes on, not knowing who e she will light next. She strikes hard, seeming to offer so much. In reality she had no firm idea of anything., Whimsy is the outer sign of her existence, as sex is its mainstay. But along the way Queenie disrupts the lives of the men with whom she comes into contact. It is important to remember that if she is treated casually, she does no harm; in fact, she gives momentary pleasure without recrimination and most

Importantly, without any demands. For Queenie playing The Sensual Game neither makes demands nor tolerates any It is difficult for some men, as it was with Karl. to believe that she is without any trace of guilt. Queeme is a real person. That. of course, is not her name. At this writing she is a show girl with a wellknown burlesque company At this writing, too, a young wouldbe film producer is trying to get her to take a part in one of his 'underground' movies. Queenie is interested only because it is a diversion. She had no drive to be a film star although this is what he promised her would happen. His line was no line at all to her. Because he cavorted with her on the floor of her'bedroom, because she allowed him to press his lips wherever he wanted, because she allowed him to act as her partner in bed he thought he had won.

In fact, however, Queenie was doing what she had subconsciously planned. There was no corntract, no firm agreement that she would make this film. Her interest would wane as soon as it was over between them. The young film tyro would be left hanging, film unshot. Queenie's rules of The Sensual Game were quite simple.

Expect nothing binding, give what you can at the time you feel like doing so. Have no hold on anyone. Admittedly the rules are onesided. But then after all, she never really promises more than she can deliver. If these rules are understood, then Queenie can be a lot of fun and games. A long step removed from The Sensual Game is one in which there is a deliberate attempt to maim, to hurt, to make men suffer physically, emotionally, and financially, singly and together. It is a game played by women who would not otherwise consider themselves ruthless.

They play it for what is often considered justified revenge. But no matter what it is called, it is devastating. If it leads to divorce exorbitant alimony may be extracted as a man's eternal penance. It may lead to murder. It has happened. It is a dangerous game, played by women in The Harassment Game.

Chapter Ten

THE HARASSMENT GAME

Selfinflicted harassment or masochism is not the issue of The Harassment Game. There are women who want to punish themselves, some physically and others by selfdeprivation, and a number who like to be verbally mistreated. As Dr Renatus Hartogs said in FourLetter Word Games, 'Only one kind of woman seems to enjoy having obscenities directed at her the severely masochistic type ... Men are usually quick to recognise and capitalise on this response. As a result, such women are particularly prone to seduction by the cruder kind of males.'

The Harassment Game, as it is generally played, is undertaken after marriage, or in some instances, after a few months of living together.

This game has been played, probably, by more women than any other. You hear it in restaurants, the theatre, or wherever couples go anywhere the man is blamed for not getting the right tickets or spending too much or too little. It is the contrary attitude a woman takes when she knows she is being overheard. It is the wife sending her husband scurrying around the supermarket for bargains, sending him out to get her ice cream or a beer. It is the wife who undresses in front of her husband, puts out the lights and goes to sleep, no matter how much he entreats her. It is the woman who knows what her body does to a man but uses its display to keep him in his place.

If it wasn't f&r the fact that the human male is barely capable of having intercourse with an uninterested and seemingly unaroused woman, the harassment game would lose most of its potential. Harassment is a game of substituted tiredness for passion, anger or pleasure. It is true as Margaret Mead wrote in Male and female, 'The human female... has gained in her control over her sexuality, and has learned to substitute many other forms of behavior for simple impulse ... the human female has learned ... to value a great variety of rewards, and fear a great variety of punishments....'

Some men might think another name for this game is nag, nag, nag. But it is much more than that. It isn't played simply to dominate the man; it is played to allow the woman to substitute another action for what is taking place. If she wants him to buy something, she can harangue him about spending too much on his car or golf clubs. The new coat for her is balm to stop the harassment. If she had brought money into the marriage, she can complain about any number of things without ever once recalling the fact that they are living on her money. She doesn't have to remind him. He knows who's wielding the big stick.

If she wants to get out once in a while, she can harass him about his coming home late, even though the reason might have been entirely legitimate. Harassment for its own sake would be a waste. It may be, on the other hand, com pensation for her own inadequacies as a cook, a housewife, or as a mistress. Harassment becomes a woman's first line of defense as she takes the offense.

Take Vem and Olive K. They had beea married for •fifteen years; each was in the middle thirties and not particularly attractive. If anything, Vem's aquiline features were more appealing than his wife's. She was an unusually thin woman, smallbreasted, narrowhipped and taken to slovenly dressing that was matched only by the careless way in which she spoke.

They lived in the old section of Baltimore, not far from U.S. 1. Vem was an assistant foreman in a wire factory. Olive worked in a bakery. He was usually home before she was through at the bakery. He got supper ready. She rituaUy cleaned up afterward. They both lapsed into silence m front of the television set. About once a week or perhaps every ten days she consented to let her husband crawl into bed with her. She made no movement to help him, allowed Sum to finish, turned over and went to sleep.

Each night Vem brought home a new idea he wanted to try out. Sometimes it was the thought of going back to school. He was told to stay where he was, he was too stupid to go back to school. Whatever the idea, it simply wouldn t work. If anyone had listened in on this couple over a period of weeks, it would have seemed impossible that they could have lived together as long as they had. let alone endure one another for a day. There just didn't seem to be one redeeming feature to their marriage.

Ask Vem about it and he'd answer, 'Oh, she's a good wife and makes a good home.' Then he'd lapse into silence.

Ask Olive about their marriage and she'd answer, 'Vem works hard but he's not too bright. Without me he would ju't be lost. Why if I hadn't found him that job he'd still be a janitor. If Vem didn't have me he'd be nothing.' And she could go on as long as one wanted to listen.

The Harassment Game, as Olive played it. was designed to keep Vem in line. She knew damn well how homely she was. She also knew her chances of ever finding another man would be pretty slim if she lost Vem. Yet, she pre ferred to harangue her husband in the belief that this would keep him. For fifteen years it worked with Vem because he never thought there might be some kind of life other than the one he had with his wife. And the strange thing was. that his wife, for all her designing, never thought there might be another kind of life for her.

Olive had, on occasion, accused Vern of making advances to a girl who worked in his company's stockroom. This wasn't true, although Vem wished she had good reason to think so. He didn't defend himself. That wasn't necessary because Olive also knew it wasn't true.

Olive and Vem had few friends. Outside of the demands Olive made on her husband, she had little else to say. Vem had long ceased to fight back. His periodic, almost daily. suggestions were only to prove that he was still alive. Sex had become something that he reached for as a thirsty man for water in the middle of the desert. He nursed the occasions carefully. They were all too short in duration. He had seen pictures of fuUbosomed women with round bottoms and welldefined legs. He may have been looking at creatures from another planet, another universe. This kind of woman existed only in his dreams, if he dared dream about them at all. On the other hand Olive was aware that men took women to the theatre and night clubs arid out dancing. But these were things one only heard about, never actually participated in. The two had successfully, it would appear, cut themselves apart from the rest of the world. Their universe was the television set, a tabloid newspaper and vice was the one bottle of beer Vern was allowed on weekends. She treated her sexual contacts with her husband with a brooding sense of responsibility. The act made her feel as if she were giving him everything. And for that, she always made the following day a hell. As Pavlov's dog soon reacted to the acid on the tongue and the food, so Vem began to await the day following each momentary evening of gratification with a distinct freezing inhibition. He didn't know whether sex with his wife was worth the verbal beat ing he would take the next day. But sex always won out.

It might have gone on that way for another fifteen years, or as long as they both stayed alive, if a change hadn't taken place in their routine. A widower who had moved in across the street asked for information about where he could find

a doctor. It seemed rather innocent. He was a big, brutallooking man. He paid no special attention to Olive. Vem was, of course, not allowed to give the stranger any information. His one attempt to do so was cut off by Olive's comment that he didn't know what he was talking about.

That night was the night for their marital consummation. It had been seven days and Vem climbed into her bed. He clumsily reached for his wife and found the washboardlike figure stiff and the ripples that were her bosom blossoming with chilling goose pimples. Vem thought this was for him. He crawled to her side of the bed. She mechanically adjusted her body, slouched into a position that made it easy for him. But then, her mood changing completely, she slapped her husband across the face destroying what had been begun, stopping with the eroelest of detours the action his body had undertaken.

'Get off, get out, who asked you?' she screamed.

She had been halfdreaming of a tall, robust man.

The next morning, more so than on any previous day. Olive made a point of telling Vem how stupid he was. how clumsy, that he had no finesse, that he would never know what to do to make. a woman happy. The poorman had expected an onslaught after a successful invasion of his wife's bed. But now the fact that she had rejected him the Eight before but continued the harassment anyway thoroughly confused him.

In this sense The Harassment Game takes on the most heinous machinations. Olive was playing it for vengeance.

She wanted to drive Vem out of the house, though not permanently. She was not secure enough, to afford that. She wanted him to leave or otherwise fight back so that she would have an excuse to act herself. She wanted Vem to get mad enough to strike her, even spend the night with another woman. That last she thought impossible.

'Don't you care,' she screamed at him, 'that you are no good as a man? Don't you care?'

He didn't answer. He was so conditioned that he heard only the sound of her voice, without really hearing the words.

'Don't you care?' she screamed again and again. When Vem didn't respond she slapped him. Her husband got off the chair, slowly picked up his things and said he was going to work.

Just before closing the front door he turned to his wife and said, his voice rising only slightly, 'You shouldn't have done that.' Before his wife could answer he was gone.

Olive had no intention of going to work. She applied touches of rouge to her cheeks, changed into her Sunday dress, put on high heels and hose, and then dashed across the street to the stranger's house,

He answered the door in his undershirt and pants.

'I, I just wanted to know if you were able to get the doctor. And I thought maybe I could help you.'

'No, I called the doctor. I mean, I don't need help.'

Olive stood in the doorway, shifting from one foot to another in the unused and uncomfortable shoes.

The man said, 'Come in!'

She went inside. He introduced himself as Ivan F.

'Excuse the place, I just moved in. Since my wife died I haven't really taken care of the furniture and things. You want some coffee? I was having some in the kitchen.'

She agreed and they went inside. Olive knew that he could not be pushed around. She wondered what it would be like to have him take her and thrust himself inside. She spilled the coffee even as she imagined being attacked by this big man.

'This is a nice place,' she said. It wasn't. It was an ugly apartment and Ivan knew it.

'Oh, that picture is so pretty,' she told him. It was a monstrosity and he knew that, too.

After a while he got up from the chair and leaning on its back said to her. 'What the hell did you come over here for? I know this is a goddam ugly place. What are you trying to do?'

'I just wanted to be helpful,' she told him. When you said you were a widower, I thought I could do something for you.'

'What do you do for that slob of a husband, that poor soul?'

Olive was indignant, 'I don't know what you mean.'

'Yes, you goddam well know. You don't dress up like this every morning. You know what, you're a driedup old prune who couldn't screw the top off a bottle.'

Olive didn't answer. She started to get up but Ivan came over 'All right, so it won't be a total loss.' He picked her up and carried her into the bedroom. There was only a mattress on the floor. 'It isn't fancy but it will do.'

He wasn't pleasant at all, nor was he tender. He ripped the dress off and laughed as he saw her try to cover up her nakedness. He didn't waste any time. He wasn't gentle. He almost broke her, split her, made her feel pain as she had never felt before. She thought her head would burst, her mouth would explode with the power of his drive. He wasted no time on tenderness. He wouldn't let her fight or move, the weight of his body rising and falling was almost too much for her to bear. She hurt all over, hoped that he would finish, that he would leave her, that she could forget him. She wondered even as he probed hard and the spit from his mouth fell on her face why she had come here. She wished for Vern, poor passive Vem who had never hurt her.

It seemed hours, rather than minutes, before he was through and standing over her, handing her her clothes and telling her he had to go to work.

Olive went home. called in sick, and went to bed. She waited for Vem's return. That evening he was late. much later than usual.

When she said he should get supper ready he told her he wasn't staying, that she could get it herself. He said, 'I've been to a lawyer.'

'What for?' But she knew the answer.

'I told him what life has been like with you and he said I could get a divorce. I could get it. That's funny. Olive. After all these years of listening to you I'm going to have the last word.' He walked over to his wife, kissed her on the forehead and when she thought he was making a joke, he said, "That is a kissoff. I read it in a book.'

If you can't stand the heat get out of the kitchen as the old warning goes. If a woman can't play the game without complaints when she loses, she shouldn't start up at all. Olive had lost. But the Harassment Game had cost Vern fifteen years of his life.

To equate harassment with sadism may not be so farfetched as it may sound. Sadism makes the infliction of pain, or any kind of physical or mental discomfort, on another person a device for achieving sexual gratification. Since harassment of a man by a woman can itself be a form of humiliation, the harassment itself may give the woman sexual pleasure.

As a woman plays The Harassment Game and drives her man away, we must assume that it gives some substitute sexual gratification. When a woman voluntarily Uves with a man who isn't her husband and proceeds to harass him continually, there would appear to be a madness to continuing the relationship.

Such was the case with Yolanda and Artie. They had been sharing the same apartment for over eight years. It was a comfortable apartment on New York's west side not pretentious but more than adequate. She was a wellpaid designer and he was a successful commercial artist. Both were sophisticated about the facts of life. On the surface 120 they arrangement was based on mutual interest in art, the theatre, music. He was thirtyfive, she three years younger. She dressed well, was tall, wellbuilt, aware of the proper uses of her body, and didn't expect Artie to be a loyal lap dog.

Artie was well over six feet, handsomely rugged, taken to drinking when not working, staying out without prior notice and couldn't believe Yolanda was capable of taking up with some other guy as long as they lived together.

Yolanda knew Artie had a line of girls who were waiting for him to move out on her. But he always came back. Yolanda had only one outlet. That was to bitch about every deal Artie made, to treat him as if he hadn't a brain in his head, was lazy and unsuccessful. All the things he was not, and they both knew it. But it provided Yolanda with an emotional outlet. More than once she changed the locks on the door to their apartment.

Not that she wanted to lock Artie out forever. It was just her way of showing him that she could have the upper hand. He'd stay away a night and come back the next day as if nothing had happened. When she wanted to make an impression she'd throw his clothes and paintings into the hall. He'd let them stay there until she had to bring them back inside. Afterward Artie might slap her across the face or he might toss her on the bed, knowing full well she would willingly melt into him, surround him with her body. She had a cute way of throwing her legs around his face, crushing him until he gasped for air, then letting go and allowing him to play with her as she played with him. They never enjoyed each other more than after one of those nights when she had locked him out. If Yolanda stopped playing The Harassment Game she was afraid they would split up. She felt more secure each year she got older, each year they stayed together.

Whenever she stopped Artie would stay away more. It was a case of them both needing each other. In their own strange way The Harassment Game kept them together, perhaps more securely than if they had been legally married. Yolanda had suggested marriage in the early years of their relationship. Artie was unconvinced it was necessary. She no longer brought the subject up. Their lives seemed eternally complete. In the suburbs of Chicago, not far from the Wisconsin border, a typical American couple live in a typical American split level with the typical two children, one dog, and one high mortgage. Their names aren't important because they are duplicated in or near every major city in the country. He gets his kicks out of risque jokes and seeing a skin flick once in a while.

He hasn't the vaguest idea of what makes his wife tick, what she needs to be fulfilled as a woman. And she, in turn, has a moralistic view of sex that completely obliterates the full purpose of their marriage. She treats her relations with her husband with the same kind of mechanical obligation as taking the kids to school or shopping in the supermarket If one asked her if she harassed her husband she would most certainly say she did not. But what else is it when she treats him as something less than a man?

She would rather have sex with a stranger, had she the nerve, than with her husband. She's no damn good in bed. She refuses to bend over backwards literally and figuratively, saying if he wants to do anything the next move will be his. Then she proceeds to put a cramp in his style by saying that what he attempts to do is disgusting. If that isn't playing The Harassment Game, what is?

This kind of woman goes about sex as would a robot. She bends her knees, uses a pillow disdainfully. Some silent voice is counting out what she should do. And she obeys. Twist here, turn there, automatically.

He takes a trip and buys a sex magazine so he can see what a real woman is like. Or else he plunks down $100.00 for a sexy Broadway musical or perhaps a burlesque show, makes a pass at a waitress. He goes on the internet and cruises for pornography.

He dreams of women he could conquer, while at home his wife attractive or not, tall or short, a woman nevertheless can give him everything he should have, should she feel the obligation to do so. That's playing The Harassment Game for sure.

The Harassment Game seems the least likely used by a woman to entrap a man. Yet it is probably the most frequently played. It can be done with all the violence and outrage of an Olive or Yolanda or with subtlety. One seem ingly contented wife, whom we shall call Natalie, was married to a young engineer. She was twentythree, had taught school for a while then stopped to live on just his salary. She was inclined to be dumpy if she didn't watch her diet, had a freckled but attractive face, and a damn good mind. Her husband, Tom, two years older, was quiet, well respected in his job, provided for her more than adequately and behaved in the most circumspect manner insofar as other women were concerned. They had moved to the out skirts of Houston from Connecticut because that was where his job took him. He gave his wife sufficient money for the house and for herself. They entertained modestly but with charm and imagination. Their friends were professionals and by and large, interesting people. Who could fault the marriage?

But listen to the little asides. Tom has eaten an hors d'oeuvre and Natalie tells him, 'You're using the wrong cracker to dip.'

Tom is sipping a high ball and Natalie tells him sweetly and just above a whisper, 'You know you can't hold your liquor, I'll have to drive home.'

Tom gets up to dance and Natalie reminds him, 'Try to do something uptodate instead of onetwo.' And she laughs at her little joke.

At home Natalie is the essence of cooperation. She never refuses Tom his place beside her. She nibbles at his ear to get him hot, offers him her full breasts, cuddles him,holds him close, whispers into his ear. Then she helps him find the way and encourages him to relax and strengthen himself so that they both may find pleasure. But in public it is something else. She cannot resist interrupting a joke he is telling to remind him o£ something someone has said. It is a constant source of amazement to their friends that they can stay together. The friends, of course, are not aware of their sexual compatibility.

Natalie plays The Harassment Game for fundamentally the same reason all other women do. It gives her a sense of fulfillment. However she is clever enough to balance it in private while publicly making him her servant With a passive husband this is possible.

Too often, though, the wife has neither the intellect nor the desire to balance at home what she does in public. One day the husband gets tired of it all and she's lost. Women are getting more selective, more careful in choosing and playing as females begin to outnumber males, as the buyer's market increases.

Now, just a word about the games men play. Whatever a man does, whatever games a man plays, it is only possible because a woman has already chosen hers. A man and a woman may 'both play a game, most often than not the same one, and equally often neither admitting that it is a game, until someone gets slapped in the face or bedded a much more satisfying conclusion.